1

RINGS

1

RINGS

Stories of the St. Louis Cardinals World Championships

JAMES RYGELSKI
ROBERT L. TIEMANN

REEDY PRESS
St. Louis, Missouri

Reedy Press
PO Box 5131
St. Louis, MO 63139, USA

Library of Congress Control Number: 2011924615

ISBN: 978-1-935806-03-5

Please visit our website at www.reedypress.com.

Cover design by Jill Halpin

Photographs on pages 2-3, 22-23, 40-41, 61, 81, 121, 147, 161 courtesy of the National Baseball Hall of Fame Library, Cooperstown, New York
Photographs on pages 184-185 courtesy of St. Louis Cardinals
Photographs on pages 5, 25, 43, 63, 83, 102-103, 105, 123, 149, courtesy of private collections
Photographs of 2006 World Series ring courtesy of Chad Blair

A special thanks to Pat Kelly with the National Baseball Hall of Fame, Paula Homan with the St. Louis Cardinals, Brad Arteaga, and Chad Blair, with assistance in illustrating the book.

Printed in the United States of America
11 12 13 14 15   5 4 3 2 1

Contents

To the family members and friends, too numerous to mention, with whom I've enjoyed watching the Cardinals in the World Series. Let's hope there are many more occasions.

—James Rygelski

To my brothers Tom and Jonathan
and to our father, who took us all to see Ken Boyer's World Series grand slam.

—Robert L. Tiemann

Introduction

"The Cardinals have tradition," Terry Cashman's popular song about them from the 1980s begins. It also states that they have a mission: "to end up in the Classic in the fall."

That's the Fall Classic, the World Series, which each October for more than a hundred years has matched the best team in the National League against the best in the American League. The St. Louis Cardinals have won it ten times, a record for any NL team. Their first world title was in 1926, the most recent in 2006.

The visible symbol of that triumph is a ring, which many players wear long after their playing days are over. "It's the proudest possession I have," said Tim McCarver, who has two of them for helping the Cardinals win the 1964 and 1967 Series. "It's fun to explain it to people," the former catcher-turned-broadcaster said when interviewed for this book.

He can explain the .478 batting average he compiled as a twenty-two-year-old in the 1964 Series, including a dramatic three-run homer that won the pivotal fifth game over the Yankees. And he can explain catching the gutsy seventh-game performances of Hall of Fame teammate Bob Gibson in both 1964 and 1967.

Even if Cardinals players don't publicly display their World Series rings, they always carry the pride of their—and, more important, their team's—accomplishments.

"You don't need a ring to remember the enjoyment of it," said former Cardinals shortstop Dal Maxvill (1964, 1967), who admits that he lost his 1964 ring while fishing with his kids and let his late father wear the other one. Maxvill's memories include playing flawlessly in the field while subbing for an injured Julian Javier at second base in 1964 then repeating a perfect fielding performance at his regular position, shortstop, in 1967.

Maxvill, later the team's general manager, was a Cardinals fan from his boyhood days in Granite City, Illinois. "When growing up you picture yourself playing in a World Series, pitching a no-hitter or hitting a home run over the fence. In my case I was lucky to live the dream and be in a few of them."

Maxvill, known mostly for his glove, ignited the winning rally for the Cardinals in 1967's seventh game when he boomed a third-inning triple off the Red Sox's ace pitcher, Jim Lonborg, after Lonborg had knocked him down with the pitch before.

Those memories of long-ago World Series games never fade for those who played them. "I'll never forget it. I wish I could do it again," Marty Marion, shortstop on the 1942–1944–1946 Cardinals world champs, recently said from his home. "I had a great time; we had such a great team." Those 1940s teams Marion played on included Hall of Famers Stan Musial and Enos Slaughter.

Marion used both glove and bat in helping the Cardinals beat the Red Sox in 1946, driving in important runs in two of the games and making a nifty catch off a toss by second baseman Red Schoendienst for a force out at second base to end the final game.

Schoendienst has Cardinals World Series rings as a player (1946), manager (1967), and coach (1964, 1982, 2006), something he takes particular pride in. "You appreciate it more the older you get because you realize then how tough it is to win a World Series," Schoendienst said after signing autographs at the January 2011 Cardinals Winter Warmup in downtown St. Louis. Never one to wear jewelry, Red said he has given his rings to "my kids."

When Schoendienst started playing, the Cardinals had to top an eight-team league, with no divisions or wild cards, to get to the World Series. When he managed, the Cardinals had to finish first in a ten-team league. When he coached in 1982, the team had to win the Eastern Division then beat the Western Division champ Atlanta Braves. And by his coaching time of 2006, the Cardinals had to top the six-team Central Division then defeat a better San Diego Padres in a best-of-five playoff and the overwhelmingly favored New York Mets in a best-of-seven series

McCarver reaffirmed the difficulty of getting to the World Series, particularly in his era, reciting a list of great players who made the Cardinals opponents, particularly from the Dodgers, Giants, and Phillies, so tough to overcome.

The World Series remains best-of-seven. Also surviving has been the Cardinals tradition of playing in it, of often battling back adversity to win it, which has been there from their first Series.

"Certainly I was aware of the tradition," current Cardinals pitcher Chris Carpenter recently said about his pitching the Redbirds to victory in 2006. He blanked the Tigers for eight innings in Game 3 as the Cardinals won to take a two games to one lead and went on to claim the title in five games.

McCarver noted that the memories go beyond the box scores and game summaries. He has particularly high regard for the character of his teammates. "It was a very intelligent, talented group of people," he said. "What gets lost in the discussion of how good of baseball players they were is the overall success they achieved after they finished playing." He noted especially teammates Gibson, Ken Boyer, Bill White, and Dick Groat.

Indeed, for both players and fans, the memories of a World Series championship never fade, as John Stuper will attest. His complete-game win in the sixth contest of the 1982 Series allowed the Cardinals to go to the seventh game, which they won. "My most lasting memory of that Series was (Cardinals closer) Bruce Sutter striking out Gorman Thomas to end it. I was a mere rookie and I was part of a World Championship team. It's sometimes hard to believe, even to this day," Stuper, now coach of the Yale University baseball team, said in an e-mail interview.

Stuper said he wears his World Series ring on special occasions, like attending a banquet. Like many former Cardinals, he comes back when he can for the mid-January Cardinals Winter Warmups in downtown St. Louis. "What brings me back? The fans. I have said it a million times. I am but a small piece of Cardinals history and these fans treat me like I am Bob Gibson. Cardinal fans are the best sports fans in the world."

10 Rings: Stories of the St. Louis Cardinals World Championships relives the hits, runs, and errors of those ten triumphant years and the fans' joy at their team's accomplishments. It also seeks to bring out the character of those players and how they handled the on- and off-field drama they faced in those seasons of glory.

1

RINGS

RUTH

1926

Cardinals Defeat Yankees 4 Games to 3

GAME 1:	CARDINALS	1	YANKEES	2
GAME 2:	CARDINALS	6	YANKEES	2
GAME 3:	CARDINALS	4	YANKEES	0
GAME 4:	CARDINALS	5	YANKEES	10
GAME 5:	CARDINALS	2	YANKEES	3
GAME 6:	CARDINALS	10	YANKEES	2
GAME 7:	CARDINALS	3	YANKEES	2

REGULAR-SEASON STARTING LINEUP		
Ray Blades	lf	.305, out with knee injury
Taylor Douthit	cf	team leader with 23 steals
Rogers Hornsby	2b	.317, down from .403 in 1925
Jim Bottomley	1b	NL-leading 120 RBIs
Billy Southworth	rf	.317
Les Bell	3b	17 HRs, 100 RBIs
Bob O'Farrell	c	NL MVP
Tommy Thevenow	ss	led all ss in plays made

PITCHERS		
Jess Haines	13-4	7-1 vs. first division teams
Flint Rhem	20-7	3.21 ERA, NL leader in wins
Willie Sherdel	16-12	3 shutouts
Vic Keen	10-9	pitched only twice in September
Art Reinhart	10-5	7-1 in last two months
Hi Bell	6-6	mop-up reliever
Grover Cleveland Alexander	9-7	waived by Cubs

BENCH	
Jake Flowers	inf
Chick Hafey	of
Wattie Holm	of
Specs Toporcer	inf

How the Cardinals Got to the World Series:

Under manager-second baseman Rogers Hornsby, the Redbirds won their first-ever pennant with an 89–65 record, finishing two games ahead of the Cincinnati Reds. The Cardinals got off to a slow start but began to jell in mid-May. Key acquisitions of outfielder Billy Southworth and pitcher Grover Cleveland Alexander in June solidified the team for its late-season run. Like many of its successors, this Cardinals championship squad played its best during the stretch drive of the final two months. Nearly the entire starting lineup had come up through the Cardinals' farm system, testifying to the success of the network of minor-league teams started by General Manager Branch Rickey in 1920.

The Cardinals' Series Opponent:

Rebounding from a seventh-place finish in 1925, the New York Yankees built a ten-game lead over the Cleveland Indians, saw it cut to two lengths in the last week of the season, but rallied to finish with a 91–63 record, three games in front at season's end. Babe Ruth also rebounded from 1925, his worst season thus far, to crack a league-leading 47 homers and 146 RBIs while batting a robust .372. The Yankees manager was Miller Huggins, who a decade before had played second base for the Cardinals while also managing them. He'd encouraged a young infielder named Rogers Hornsby.

Painting the Town Red—the First Time

The St. Louis Cardinals had their doubters as they prepared to face the mighty New York Yankees in the first game of the 1926 World Series. One of them was a New York City cop who reportedly wouldn't let Cardinals manager Rogers Hornsby and his squad enter Yankee Stadium for the Series opener, thinking they were fans trying to pull a fast one.

"Is that so?" the disbelieving policeman told Hornsby when he introduced himself and his team at the players' entrance. "Run along now. . . . You can't stand here."

Fortunately, Lou Gehrig, the Yankees young slugging first baseman, arrived at that time and verified his opponents' identities for the man in blue.

The 1926 World Series, the first for the Cardinals, followed a tight National League pennant race in which St. Louis finished two games ahead of the Cincinnati Reds. That the Cardinals, who'd finished fourth the year before and never higher than third place, would play in the World Series may have surprised many veteran baseball watchers before the 1926 season began.

But not Hornsby.

During the Cardinals' spring training in San Antonio, Texas, Hornsby, also the team's starting second baseman and an eleven-year veteran of the team, had told his charges that anyone who didn't believe the Cardinals could win the pennant should pick up his pay and leave immediately. None did. He told the players not to brag about their potential but to simply go out and show it. After a so-so start, they did.

Most of these young players—thirteen of whom had been born since 1900, making the Cardinals one of the youngest major-league teams—had come through the Cardinals' own "farm" system. That network of minor-league teams that the Cardinals had either full or majority ownership of had been devised by General Manager Branch Rickey six years before. Before 1920, when all minor-league teams were independently owned, the Cardinals were often outbid by wealthier major-league clubs for talented youngsters gaining seasoning in the minors. The Cardinals' farm system evened the score for the poorer Redbirds and returned the highest dividends in 1926.

Such players as first baseman "Sunny" Jim Bottomley, who wore his cap cocked to one side; slick-fielding shortstop Tommy Thevenow; third baseman Lester Bell; leadoff man and left fielder Ray Blades; Chick Hafey, the first bespectacled outfielder in baseball history; speedy center fielder Taylor Douthit; as well as hard-throwing, and harder drinking, pitcher Flint Rhem and fellow moundsman "Wild" Bill Hallahan had all spent time in the Cardinals' minor-league system.

The Yankees took the opposite approach to player development. Colonel Jacob Ruppert simply opened his checkbook and bought the best players he could. Among them had been Babe Ruth, purchased from the Boston Red Sox for the then-extravagant sum of $125,000 the same year Rickey began the Cardinals' farm system. Yankees general manager Ed Barrow, later called "the builder of baseball's greatest empire" by Gehrig, also found Boston willing to trade to the Yankees such pitchers as Herb Pennock and Waite Hoyt. After the 1925 season, Ruppert shelled out a lot of money to sign minor league second baseman Tony Lazzeri, who had hit

60 homers and driven in 222 runs for the Salt Lake City Bees that year. All of them would play critical roles in returning the Yankees to the top of the American League in 1926 after the club's disastrous seventh-place finish the year before.

If there was one connection between the Cardinals and Yankees, it was Yankees manager Miller Huggins. Huggins had played second base for the Cardinals and managed the team a decade before; he then moved on to manage the Yankees in 1918 after a failed bid to buy the Cardinals. Huggins had nurtured Rogers Hornsby when the young Texan first came up in 1915 as a gangly shortstop who had trouble hitting. When Huggins told Hornsby he was going to be farmed out, meaning sent to the minors for more experience, the then-naïve Hornsby said he could instead work on a relative's farm. Huggins, who never married but wished he'd been able to have a family, went on to be a father figure to such young Yankees as Gehrig and Lazzeri.

Ruth and Hornsby were the top two sluggers at that time and were photographed together several times in Yankee Stadium before the Series opener. Coming off his worst season in 1925, and thought by many to be washed up at age thirty-one, Ruth vowed to come back in 1926—and he did, big time. He led the AL with 47 homers and 146 RBIs while finishing second in the batting race at .372. One big change for Ruth was his patching up the rocky relationship he'd had with Huggins, who'd fined and suspended him the year before—reportedly reminding Ruth in a paternal way of his great potential. Hornsby was hobbled by injuries—most notably a baseline collision with a Reds player—but still played in 134 games. He continued to zealously guard his eyesight by not going to any picture shows, as the silent movies in theaters were then called, and not reading much more than the racing odds printed in newspapers. Hornsby's average "slipped" to .317 from .403 the year before, when he'd won his second triple crown. Still, he remained the favorite of Cardinals fans because of his status as a perennial batting champ who had cleared the .400 mark three times. He was also a fan favorite because of his managerial success begun the previous year when Cardinals owner Sam Breadon named Hornsby to replace Rickey as field boss on Memorial Day with the team in last place. Hornsby pulled the team up to fourth by season's end.

On the field, Hornsby was boss, and his players knew that, but to a man they said they liked his tough but fair style. Hornsby's managerial approach, noted the *Sporting News*, was the opposite of his predecessor. Rickey had been, in Breadon's words, a "goddamned Sunday school teacher," with a daily instructional blackboard presentation in the clubhouse. A catcher-outfielder-first baseman with an unspectacular .239 career average over four seasons with the Browns and Yankees, Rickey nonetheless was an outstanding judge of baseball talent who also insisted his players follow a myriad of rules both on and off the field. Hornsby made his rules as simple as possible: Play your best all the time. He would fine players who didn't. He kept to a minimum the signs relayed by the manager and coaches to the players on the field. And he would not platoon his players, saying that a good left-handed hitter should be able to hit a left-handed pitcher. Keeping such a hitter on the bench would only lessen the man's confidence, Hornsby told the writer F. C. Lane.

Breadon, a successful St. Louis auto dealer who'd grown up in New York, returned Rickey to the general manager's post, a job for which he was better suited. While some animosity remained, the Breadon–Rickey–Hornsby triumvirate seemed to be in harmony as the 1926 season progressed. Near midseason, they realized that while the kids they had were now ready, the team needed the stability of a veteran. When New York Giants manager John McGraw offered outfielder Billy Southworth for Cardinals outfielder Heine Mueller, the St. Louis brass agreed it was a good deal. It was, for Southworth hit a steady .317 for the Cardinals the rest of the way. When the Cubs put veteran pitcher Grover Cleveland Alexander on waivers in late June—because Manager Joe McCarthy thought

Alexander was a bad influence on the Cubs' youngsters—Cardinals leadership again decided it would be a good addition. "Ol' Pete," as Alexander was known, steadied both the starting staff and the bullpen, winning nine games for the Redbirds. The man who would go on to win 373 games in his career, tied for third-best in major league history, was in good company: Cardinals coach Bill Killefer had been Alex's catcher when he'd first broken in with the Phillies in 1911 and when both had been traded to the Cubs; Cardinals starting catcher Bob O'Farrell had also caught Alexander in Chicago. They knew of his epilepsy and his alcoholism.

An amateur psychologist, Hornsby noted that his players were paying too much attention to the scores of their closest competitors, the Reds and Pirates, as displayed on the outfield scoreboard during the last week of the season. So he prevailed upon the scoreboard operators at the Polo Grounds in New York to keep the Cincinnati game off the board while the Cardinals were playing the Giants. The scoreboard operator complied and the Cardinals, without the distraction, concentrated solely on beating the Giants—and clinching the NL pennant that day.

Having played their last twenty-five regular-season games on the road, the Cardinals found they had to open the World Series with a pair of games in Yankee Stadium. Many professional oddsmakers listed the Yankees as favorites, some by as much as 15–1, though the Cardinals had their share of supporters among the press. The Cardinals had drawn over 37,000 for a game in Sportsman's Park in St. Louis, but that was nothing compared to 61,658 that filled majestic Yankee Stadium for the first game on Saturday, October 2. "You count 'em upstairs and I'll count 'em downstairs and we'll see how much money we're gonna make," pitcher Bill Sherdel told third baseman Lester Bell during the team's warm-ups before the first game.

The Cardinals seemed intent on proving that they were the Yankees' equals by scoring a run in the very first inning of the opener. Douthit led off with a double and scored on a bloop two-out single by Bottomley. But as Gehrig had led the Cardinals into the park after their run-in with the cop, he led the Yankees to victory, grounding out to drive in the tying run in the first and singling home the eventual winning run in the sixth. After getting two hits off Pennock in the first, the Cardinals managed only one more safety and lost the opener 2–1. Sherdel gave up six hits and seemed to have found his groove until giving up the lead in the sixth.

Newspapers at that time featured analyses under the bylines of Hornsby, Ruth, McGraw, and others, though penned for them by various sportswriters. Hornsby boasted that the Cardinals were "going to knock the Yankees out of their mitts" while Ruth predicted that Yankees pitchers would stop the Cardinals' "swing hitters," as he called the era's power hitters.

The second game, played before a then-Series record attendance of 63,600, set a pattern other Cardinals Series teams would follow: winning convincingly after dropping the opener. It also gave Alexander the chance to show that he still had the skills he'd displayed in the 1915 Series while pitching for the Phillies against the Red Sox.

However, Alexander got off to a rocky start when he gave up an RBI single to Lazzeri in the second then intercepted a throw during a double-steal attempt meant to cut down Lazzeri coming home and threw it into left field on the attempted rundown, allowing him to score.

The Cardinals came right back, as the first two men singled off Yankees starter Urban Shocker, and Hornsby moved them over with a sacrifice bunt. Bottomley drove home both to tie the score at 2–2.

Alexander had given up three hits in the Yankees' second. But from then on he was virtually untouchable, surrendering only a leadoff single in the third before retiring the next twenty-one straight batters. He told reporters afterward that it had been the first time he had pitched in twelve days and that he had some trouble getting loose in the beginning of the contest. Once limbered, he said, "I had control as good as I've ever had."

While Alexander was mowing down the Yankees one-two-three every inning, Shocker was keeping the Cardinals at bay. That is, until the seventh when Southworth, who'd played before New York fans the first half of the season as a Giant and received a nice ovation from them in the first game, stroked a two-out, three-run homer to break the game open. In the ninth, Thevenow, the normally light-hitting shortstop, skied the ball toward right field. Ruth lunged at it, missed, then momentarily lost the ball's location despite immense help given him by fans in that section. By the time Ruth grabbed it and threw it in, Thevenow had scampered around the bases for an inside-the-park homer that merely iced the Cardinals 6–2 win and sent the Series back to St. Louis squared at one game each.

In the first decade of radio broadcasts—but two decades before TV and a couple generations before pitchers took forever to pitch and batters stepped out of the box between every delivery—each of the first two games had taken less than two hours to play.

Cardinals fans hadn't seen their heroes since the first day of September, when the club completed its home schedule. But they turned out in tremendous numbers for a motorcade through downtown St. Louis on that Monday, a scheduled off day to allow for travel between New York and St. Louis. A *Globe-Democrat* headline on a story about the parade stated, "Frenzied multitudes lionize their baseball heroes." The story said Hornsby rode with his wife while carrying their infant son, Billy. "A more popular figure never passed through the streets of St. Louis," it noted.

Field-level box seats added for the Series near the dugouts boosted Sportsman's Park seating capacity but virtually cut off the players' views from their benches of balls hit near the foul lines. However, the view the Cardinals had from their bench was a pleasing one, as it was for the 37,708 fans who filled the park. Jesse Haines, the Cardinals knuckleballing right-hander, who'd pitched the last inning of the opener, started the third contest and continued the mastery Alexander had finished with the game before. After Haines retired the first six Yankee hitters in a row, newspapers noted that Cardinals moundsmen had pitched the equivalent of a perfect game by retiring twenty-seven straight batters.

After Thevenow drove in a run on a force out at second in the home half of the fourth—and reached safely as Yankee shortstop Mark Koenig threw the ball away trying to complete a double play that would have nullified the run—Haines added a couple more runs by homering into the right-field pavilion. "Pop," as the thirty-three-year-old Haines was called, limited the Yankees to five hits and three walks, completing a 4–0 whitewashing in one hour, forty-one minutes.

Cardinals fans could be excused for thinking their team would soon wrap up the Series. The Redbirds could do no wrong while the Yankees looked dead. And there was no reason to think otherwise when Flint Rhem, the Cardinals twenty-game winner that season, struck out the first two Yankees hitters by making them chase breaking balls off the outside corner. Rhem, from Rhems, South Carolina, a town named for his family, was one of the more colorful characters on the club. Rhem had gotten drunk one night saying he was trying to keep Alexander from getting his hands on the whiskey bottle. But after his sober start against the Yankees leadoff men, Rhem got intoxicated with the notion of how to pitch to Babe Ruth. Ruth strode to the plate a .200 hitter for the first three games. Hornsby had told his hurlers to pitch to Ruth but not give him anything he could handle.

Rhem challenged Ruth with a fastball over the plate, and Ruth belted it well beyond the right-field pavilion to give the Yankees a 1–0 lead.

The Cardinals tied the contest in their half of the second as

Douthit and Southworth singled, and Hornsby followed with a base hit, driving in his first run of the Series.

Ruth gave the Yankees a 2–1 lead in the third by hitting another Rhem fastball out of the park in deep right center. They added a solo run on a double by third baseman Joe Dugan in the fourth.

The Babe had been a great pitcher before being converted, primarily for his slugging, to an outfielder. But many people overlooked his fielding and throwing. In the first game he had robbed Bob O'Farrell, the Cardinals catcher, by spearing a line drive headed for the right-center-field gap. In the bottom of the fourth of the fourth game, Ruth's left arm reinforced his defensive prowess.

The Cardinals rallied with three runs to take a 4–3 lead and might have had more except Ruth charged a two-out single by Southworth and threw a strike to the plate to nail Douthit trying to score from second. Yankees shortstop Koenig then made up for his error in the previous inning by doubling in the tying mark as the Yankees plated four to take a 7–4 lead.

Ruth put the game out of reach the next inning by hitting probably the longest home run in Sportsman's Park history, a massive two-run shot to deep center field off a changeup from reliever Art Reinhart, estimated at 475 feet on the fly. Ruth showed that he could take advantage of the 315-foot right field line, the 354-foot right-center barrier, and the 426-foot center-field wall. When he trotted out to his left-field position, even partisan Cardinals fans—as they still do—showed their appreciation of the opponent's Herculean effort with applause.

The *Sporting News* reported: "The folks in the grandstand were inclined to be a bit conservative. A few bitter-enders committed the *lese-majeste* (offense against a ruler) of booing the king, but out in the bleachers it was all tumult and uproar. The boys in the sun seats in left, where Ruth was stationed, got to their feet as if one man. They waved papers and programs and Cardinal banners and tossed a few ancient straw hats out on the field."

After the game, Hornsby criticized Rhem and Reinhart for putting the ball "over the plate so he (Ruth) could have a little practice socking the ball over the fence." Hornsby added that Haines and Alexander certainly had known not to pitch Ruth that way.

For the third day in a row, Cardinals fans set a Sportsman's Park attendance record as 39,552 came to the October 7 contest, the last in St. Louis. It was a rematch of the opener in which Pennock had bested Sherdel 2–1. Going into the ninth, it looked like the Cardinals southpaw would return the favor, leading by that same score. But Gehrig led off with a double and Lazzeri reached on a bunt single. Today, a manager would probably summon a reliever, but in those days managers often stuck longer—not just with starters but just about any moundsman. The Cardinals had led the NL with ninety complete games, and Hornsby let Sherdel stay. Pinch-hitter Ben Paschal tied the game with a single, and in the tenth inning, Lazzeri hit a sacrifice fly off Sherdel to give the Yankees a 3–2 lead. Pennock gave up a single in the tenth but stymied the Cardinals to give the Yankees a three-games-to-two lead going back to New York.

In New York, the weekend promised to be a rainy one, which may have held attendance for the sixth game down to 48,615 from its 60,000-plus for each of the first two games. Alexander got the start this time and pitched another complete-game victory, 10–2. Cardinal batters made it easy for him by jumping on Yankees starter Bob Shawkey for three runs in the first and putting the game away with five more in the seventh. Alexander gave up eight hits and two walks but pitched around his mistakes. The game required only two hours and five minutes.

The stage was set for the seventh game on Sunday, October 10, one of the finest clinchers not just in Cardinals history but in all the annals of the Fall Classic.

Threat of rain again may have kept the crowd down, as only 38,093 showed up to watch the Cardinals' Jesse Haines, of the home-run-shutout fame in game three, face the Yankees' Waite Hoyt, who had benefitted from Ruth's three circuit blasts to win Game 4.

Ruth got the scoring going in the bottom of the third. Haines had struggled in the first two frames, stranding two runners in the first and another in the second. He appeared to be breezing, though, in the third, having retired the first two men when Ruth lifted one of his knuckleballs over the wall in right center for a 1–0 New York lead.

Showing the resiliency that all champions must have, however, the Cardinals came right back the next inning. Bottomley singled with one out and might have been wiped out when Bell followed with a ground ball in the hole at short. But Mark Koenig—in the lineup primarily for his bat—booted it, allowing both runners to reach safely. It was Koenig's fourth error of the Series; his miscue in the third game had kept an inning alive and allowed Haines an at-bat in which he'd homered, while two other Koenig errors came in Yankee wins.

Hafey blooped a single to left in front of Meusel, loading the bases. Then came the crucial play: O'Farrell lofted a fly ball to left, and the normally sure-handed Meusel dropped it, allowing the tying run to score and keeping the bases loaded. Up came Thevenow, a shortstop in the lineup primarily because of his glove. He'd singled in the first, pushing his average over the .400 mark for the games and leading all Series hitters. Now he measured a Hoyt pitch and smacked it into right, scoring Hafey and O'Farrell—unearned runs but ones that counted nonetheless in giving the Cardinals a 3–1 lead.

Back in St. Louis, the *Post-Dispatch* reported, many people were gathered in homes and having "radio parties" while listening to the progress of the game over that still-new medium. The *Post-Dispatch*, self-servingly, noted that its own station, KSD, was carrying the feed of New York's WEAF and the tones of Graham McNamee, one of baseball's first great radio play-by-play men. As

Thevenow had helped the Cardinals with his bat, he did so with his glove in the bottom of the fourth. With Lou Gehrig on second and two out, Yankees catcher Henry Severeid lashed a vicious liner over the shortstop's head. Here's what McNamee's call sounded like to the ears of Cardinals and Yankees fans:

> *"The first pitch—oh, oh boy, oh boy, I hope to tell you Thevenow made a catch! Oh, what a catch of Severeid's liner. It was ten feet up if it was an inch and it started to go by shortstop. Thevenow—I now know, I suspected it before, but I now know that he wears springs in the bottom of his shoes. He went up in the air four feet. He was up so high it took him about ten seconds to drop."*

Then the Cardinals' offense took the rest of the day off. Pop wasn't as domineering as he'd been in the third game in St. Louis, but he pitched around the hits and walks he gave to the Yankees, as Alexander had the day before. The Yankees reached him for a run in the sixth on a two-out single by third baseman Joe Dugan and a double by catcher Henry Severeid.

The Yankees in their seventh, however, threatened. Combs led off with a single and was sacrificed to second. Ruth was intentionally walked, one of four free passes he would receive this day. Meusel forced the Babe at second, but Gehrig walked to fill the bases for Lazzeri. The crowd started chanting, "Push 'em up," the nickname given the young RBI producer.

What happened next has developed its own legend over the decades, as people who weren't at the scene have augmented the story. For the truth, we can trust the written account of an eyewitness, Les Bell, the Cardinals third baseman.

Hornsby came to the mound and found the fingers of Haines' pitching hand bleeding from where he had rubbed off the skin throwing his knuckleball. Haines said he could throw fastballs but no longer the knuckler, but Hornsby didn't want to feed Lazzeri fast ones, so he summoned Alexander from the right-field bullpen. He had told Alexander after winning the day before to be ready to relieve. Alexander said he was prepared "to pitch my arm off to win the championship for St. Louis" but added that he wouldn't take any unnecessary warm-ups.

Rumor has always had it that Alexander was either drunk or hungover in the bullpen. Bell called such charges "a lot of bunk." The Cardinals pitcher later swore that he was neither, though he did acknowledge that he and his wife, Amy, had had a drink the night before. The "long and lanky . . . old Nebraskan," as Bell called him, ambled in wearing the long wool sweater favored by teams of the era, then handed it to a teammate before meeting Hornsby on the mound. Alexander had already practiced a little psychology by coming in so slowly, knowing that it would rattle the young Lazzeri, who was anxious to hit.

Alexander outlined his plan: Throw an inside fastball then pitch him outside off the plate. Hornsby first objected, but Alexander assured his manager that if Lazzeri hit the inside pitch it would go foul.

And that's what happened: Lazzeri lined one foul down the left-field line that just missed being a grand slam, then he struck out chasing balls off the outside corner. Alexander slowly walked in from the field and sat down on the bench, accepting gratitude from his teammates then asking them to leave him alone to think about how he was going to pitch the last two innings.

He had no trouble with the Yankees in the eighth or with the first two hitters in the ninth. But then he walked Ruth, just missing the corner on a 3–2 pitch. To the surprise of everyone, with Meusel at bat, Ruth tried to steal second. Hornsby was waiting with O'Farrell's throw and put it on the sliding Ruth.

The Cardinals were champions of the world. Back home, people poured into the streets and partied for the rest of the day, well into the evening, and even the next morning in some places.

The Cardinals returned to Sportsman's Park the next night, the ballpark illuminated by temporary floodlights, to the cheers of their adoring fans. Hornsby, most popular of them all, wasn't present, since he returned to Texas to bury his mother. Before her death she had reportedly told him he shouldn't worry about burying her remains until the World Series had concluded.

A few days before Christmas, the tension that had mostly stayed beneath the surface between Breadon and Hornsby erupted. Breadon had argued for Hornsby when he had been overlooked in the Most Valuable Player voting in 1924, then expressed satisfaction when Hornsby had won the vote in 1925. Hornsby had berated Breadon in front of the team when he told the owner that he wouldn't send his starters to play an exhibition game Breadon had arranged on an off-day in September.

When Hornsby demanded a three-year salary at $50,000 per season, Breadon said he would give only one year at that price. The two had a shouting match in Breadon's office, and after Hornsby stormed out, Breadon took a drink to settle his nerves then called Charles Stoneham, owner of the New York Giants. The two exchanged second basemen—Hornsby going to New York for the Giants' Frankie Frisch and pitcher Jimmy Ring.

Irate fans teepeed Breadon's house and flooded his home with threatening phone calls. The St. Louis Chamber of Commerce passed a resolution condemning the trade.

The Cardinals finished second to the Pirates the next season while taking their second pennant in 1928, with Frisch showing he was more than capable at filling Hornsby's place at second base. Cardinals fans have their heroes, but the hurt at losing them always is soothed by future pennants and World Series appearances.

1926 Line Scores

Game 1, Saturday, October 2, at Yankee Stadium, New York

	1 2 3 4 5 6 7 8 9	R	H	E
St. Louis	1 0 0 0 0 0 0 0 0	1	3	1
New York	1 0 0 0 0 1 0 0 x	2	6	0

W—Pennock L—Sherdel
Time—1:48 Attendance—61,658

Summary: After jumping to 1–0 lead on Taylor Douthit's leadoff double and Jim Bottomley's two-out single, Cardinals bats managed but one hit against Yankees southpaw Herb Pennock while Lou Gehrig drove in both runs for a New York victory.

Game 2, Sunday, October 3, at Yankee Stadium

	1 2 3 4 5 6 7 8 9	R	H	E
St. Louis	0 0 2 0 0 0 3 0 1	6	12	1
New York	0 2 0 0 0 0 0 0 0	2	4	0

W—Alexander L—Shocker
Time—1:57 Attendance—63,600

Summary: Billy Southworth's two-out, three-run homer in the seventh broke tie and propelled Cardinals to Series-evening win. Grover Cleveland Alexander went distance, retiring last 21 straight.

Game 3, Tuesday, October 5, at Sportsman's Park, St. Louis

	1 2 3 4 5 6 7 8 9	R	H	E
New York	0 0 0 0 0 0 0 0 0	0	5	1
St. Louis	0 0 0 3 1 0 0 0 x	4	8	0

W—Haines L—Ruether
Time—1:41 Attendance—37,708

Summary: Jesse Haines turned in second straight route-going performance for Cardinals, never allowing a Yankee past second base. Cards hurler also hit two-run homer in fourth after Redbirds scored first run on throwing error by Yankees shortstop Mark Koenig.

Game 4, Wednesday, October 6, at Sportsman's Park

	1 2 3 4 5 6 7 8 9	R	H	E
New York	1 0 1 1 4 2 1 0 0	10	14	1
St. Louis	1 0 0 3 0 0 0 0 1	5	14	0

W—Hoyt L—Reinhart
Time—2:38 Attendance—38,825

Summary: Babe Ruth battered Cardinals pitchers Flint Rhem for two homers that landed on Grand Boulevard and Lester Bell for another to dead center as Yankees erased early Redbird lead to knot Series.

Game 5, Thursday, October 7, at Sportsman's Park

	1	2	3	4	5	6	7	8	9	10	R	H	E
New York	0	0	0	0	0	1	0	0	1	1	3	9	1
St. Louis	0	0	0	1	0	0	1	0	0	0	2	7	1

W—Pennock L—Sherdel
Time—2:28 Attendance—39,552

Summary: Bill Sherdel's wild pitch in 10th helped Yankees to push across winning run on flyball by Tony Lazzeri. Cardinals carried lead into the ninth, but three straight Yankee hits helped send game into extra innings.

Game 6, Saturday, October 9, at Yankee Stadium

	1	2	3	4	5	6	7	8	9	R	H	E
St. Louis	3	0	0	0	1	0	5	0	1	10	13	2
New York	0	0	0	1	0	0	1	0	0	2	8	1

W—Alexander L—Shawkey
Time—2:05 Attendance—48,615

Summary: Cardinals jumped on starter Bob Shawkey for three first-inning runs, and Alexander again throttled Yankees offense, setting stage for deciding seventh game.

Game 7, Sunday, October 10, at Yankee Stadium

	1	2	3	4	5	6	7	8	9	R	H	E
St. Louis	0	0	0	3	0	0	0	0	0	3	8	0
New York	0	0	1	0	0	1	0	0	0	2	8	3

W—Haines L—Hoyt
Time—2:15 Attendance—38,093

Summary: Cardinals won first World Championship in nail-biter before crowd held down by threatening rainy weather. Two-run single by light-hitting shortstop Tommy Thevenow gave Redbirds lead for good in third. Grover Cleveland Alexander, following a complete game the day before, came out of bullpen to fan Yanks' rookie sensation Tony Lazzeri with bases loaded and two out in seventh. Alexander then retired five more until Babe Ruth walked with two out but was gunned out trying to steal second base.

Total attendance: 328,051
Total gate receipts: $1,207,864, a record at that time and not exceeded until 1936.
Cardinals player's share: $5,584.51

1931

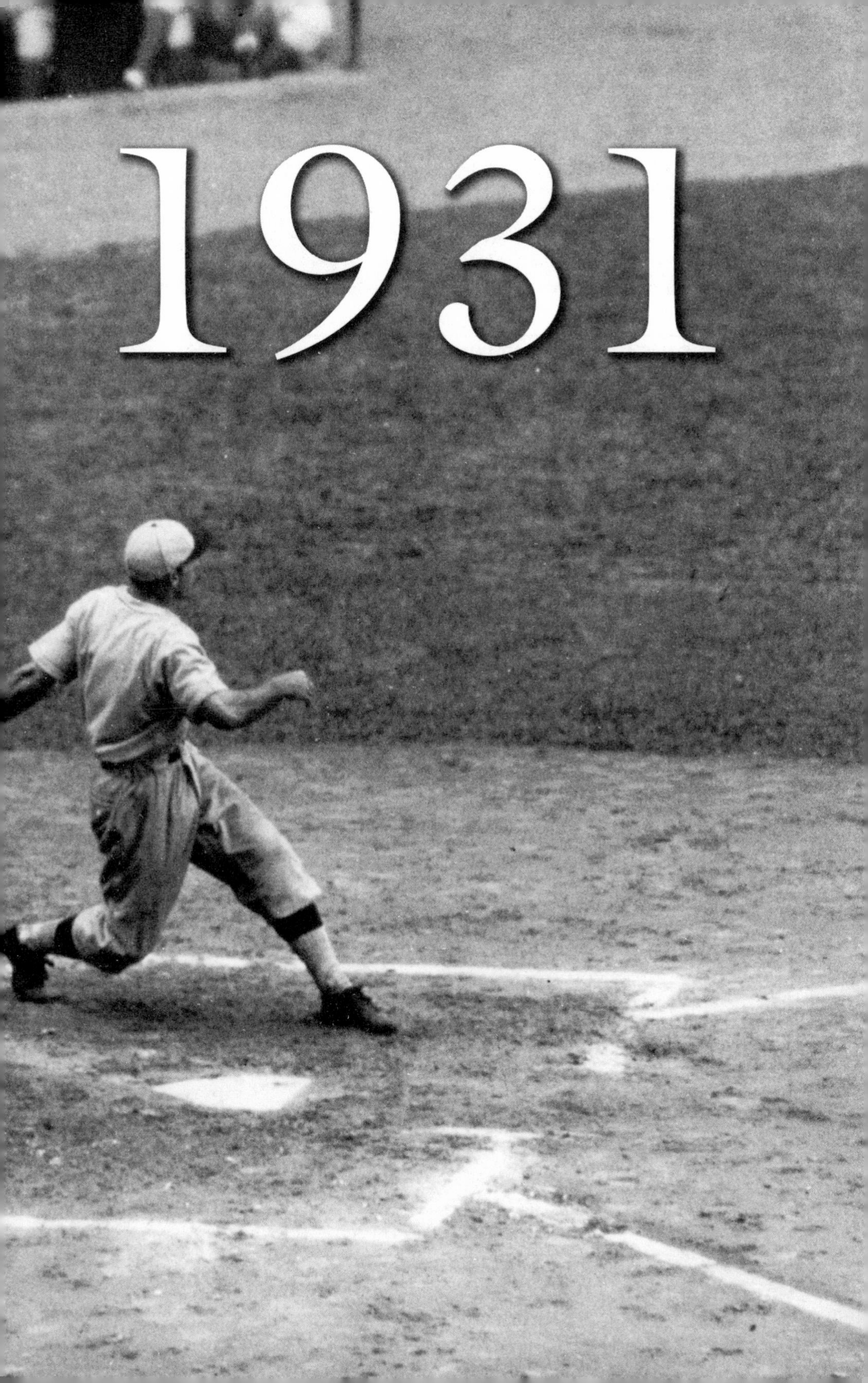

Cardinals Defeat Athletics 4 Games to 3

GAME 1:	CARDINALS	2	ATHLETICS	6
GAME 2:	CARDINALS	2	ATHLETICS	0
GAME 3:	CARDINALS	5	ATHLETICS	2
GAME 4:	CARDINALS	0	ATHLETICS	3
GAME 5:	CARDINALS	5	ATHLETICS	1
GAME 6:	CARDINALS	1	ATHLETICS	8
GAME 7:	CARDINALS	4	ATHLETICS	2

REGULAR-SEASON STARTING LINEUP		
Sparky Adams	3b	.293, 97 runs
George Watkins	rf	.288, 13 HRs, 13 triples
Frank Frisch	2b	.311, NL MVP
Jim Bottomley	1b	.348
Chick Hafey	lf	NL batting champ at .349
Pepper Martin	cf	.300
Jimmie Wilson	c	.274
Charley Gelbert	ss	.289

PITCHERS		
Bill Hallahan	19–9	159 Ks, led NL
Paul Derringer	18–8	.692 winning percentage
Burleigh Grimes	17–9	17 complete games
Syl Johnson	11–9	3.00 ERA
Flint Rhem	11–10	3.56 ERA
Jess Haines	12–3	out with sore shoulder

BENCH	
Jake Flowers	inf
Andy High	inf
Rip Collins	inf
Ernie Orsatti	of

How the Cardinals Got to the World Series:

St. Louis won its second straight pennant under Manager Gabby Street. It was also the Cardinals' fourth National League title in six years, but the first that came easily. They took over first place to stay on Memorial Day and finished thirteen games ahead of the second-place New York Giants.

The Cardinals' Series Opponent:

The Philadelphia Athletics were managed by the legendary Connie Mack. The Tall Tactician, age sixty-eight, completed his thirty-first season at the helm of the A's by attaining his ninth—and last—pennant, though he would manage the club through the 1950 season. They had won 107 games to cop the AL pennant by 13½ lengths and became the first team in big-league history to win more than 100 games for three consecutive seasons. Having won the Series in 1929 and 1930, they were looking to become the first club ever to win three consecutive modern World Championships.

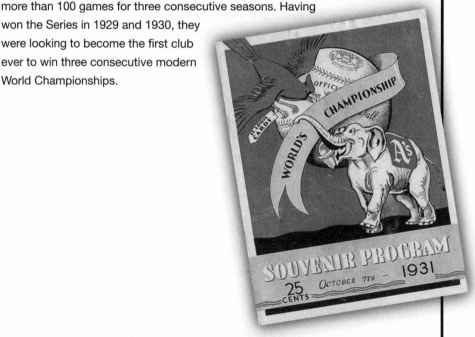

Confluence of Talent Outplays the Mighty A's

With two out in the ninth inning of Game 7 of the 1931 World Series, "Old Stubbebeard," Burleigh Grimes, trudged off the mound at Sportsman's Park, physically and emotionally spent in his effort to win the World Championship for his Cardinals teammates. For the second time in the series, he had squelched the mighty Philadelphia Athletics lineup. But with two on and a 4–2 lead, the veteran spitballer was so tired he "could barely drag one foot after the other." It would be up to younger men to finish off the A's.

The 1931 Cardinals were awash with talent, both young and old. Captain Frank Frisch, in his thirteenth year in the majors, was voted the National League's Most Valuable Player. Pepper Martin, who had finally been made a starting player in midseason, had such an astounding World Series that he was named "Athlete of the Year" by the Associated Press. Rookie Paul Derringer finished 18–8 to lead the league's pitchers in winning percentage, while "Wild" Bill Hallahan, who had debuted for the Redbirds in 1925, tied for the NL lead in wins with 19, strikeouts with 159, and—living up to his nickname—bases on balls with 115.

"Sunny" Jim Bottomley, a regular since 1923, was challenged for the first base job by James "Rip" Collins, who had been idling on the Cardinals' Rochester farm team for the better part of five seasons. Catcher Gus Mancuso, age twenty-five, had hit .366 in half-time duty in 1930 yet could not win the starting job from thirty-one-year-old veteran Jimmie Wilson. When stellar third-year shortstop Charley Gelbert was injured in July, the Cardinals plucked old friend Jake Flowers off the waiver wire to fill in. Jake had originally come up as a Cardinal in 1923.

Branch Rickey's farm system was producing an excess of players, already having produced one World Series champ and two other pennant winners. In 1931, counting leadoff man Sparky Adams, who had made it to the majors with the Cubs but had been groomed in the Cardinals minor-league system beforehand, three of the four starting infielders, all three of the starting outfielders, and two of the top three winners on the pitching staff had come up through Rickey's system.

St. Louis took over first place for good on Memorial Day and finished the season with 101 wins, becoming the first NL team in eighteen years to reach the one hundred mark in victories. New York finished a distant second, thirteen games behind. These Cardinals had everything. As Manager Gabby Street recalled years later, "I've seen a lot of great ball clubs in my day, but for pitching, hitting, spirit, and all-around balance, I would back my 1931 Cardinal team against any of them." Confidence was a big part of their game, and they wound up 29–16 in one-run games, the best in the league, and a remarkable record for a runaway pennant winner.

But the season was not without its tribulations. Everyone in the starting lineup missed at least a week at some point. It started with slugging left fielder Chick Hafey, who held out all through spring training before agreeing to a $12,500 contract ten days after the regular season began. Rickey insisted that the salary was for the full season and docked Hafey for games missed. Another ten days passed before Hafey finally signed the deal. Then Rickey sent him to Danville to get in playing condition by working out with the Cardinals farm team in the Illinois–Indiana–Iowa (Three-Eye)

League. By the time he finally debuted on May 16, Hafey had lost out on $2,100 of his raise. Livid with Rickey, Chick vented his frustrations at bat, copping the NL batting title.

Hafey's absence didn't stop the team from starting 14–4, and it created playing time for Martin, a hard-sliding speedster who loved to play all out. When Pepper went back to bench duty he boiled over with desire to get back out there. Beside himself, he barged in on Vice President Rickey and pleaded his case. The executive outwardly counseled patience but was convinced he had to make room for the irrepressible Oklahoman. At the June 15 trading deadline, Rickey dealt Taylor Douthit, the mainstay center fielder for three Cardinals pennant winners, and Martin was installed in his stead.

Bottomley, another Cardinals mainstay, suffered a hip injury in early June. Collins stepped right into the cleanup spot and delivered numerous big hits. When Sunny Jim was healthy again, young Rip's bat stayed in the lineup. Bottomley did not get the job back until Collins chipped a bone in his ankle in early August. Not wanting to give it back, the veteran hit .383 in August and .368 in September, and Collins remained a bench man after his injury healed.

Perhaps no game summed up the Cardinals regular season better than September 16, the day they clinched the pennant. The Redbirds were tied with the Phillies, 2–2, when word arrived in the dugout that the Giants had lost in Cincinnati and the Cardinals had mathematically clinched the flag. Street then took out all eight of his starting position players in the second half of the game and let the replacements roll over the Phils for a 6–3 win.

While the Cardinals were definitely the big dogs in the National League, they were distinct underdogs in the World Series against Connie Mack's Philadelphia Athletics. Having won more than one hundred AL games for the third year in a row, the A's were trying to become the first team ever to win three straight World Series titles. They looked unstoppable, headed by Lefty Grove's 31–4 pitching record and Al Simmons' .390 batting. Moreover, Philadelphia was at full strength and healthy, while the Cardinals were a little short, with leadoff man Adams hobbling on a sprained ankle and twelve-game winner Jess Haines out with a sore shoulder.

Even during the Depression, the Cardinals showed a 100,000 increase in attendance for 1931, to 608,535. The A's, winning their third straight pennant, showed the same dwindling fan support as had Mack's other dynasty, the 1910–14 club that won four pennants; 1931's attendance was down to 627,464, more than 200,000 less than the 1929 club had drawn.

Philadelphia had handled a surging Cardinals club in the 1930 Series, winning in six games, so most people expected them to win again. The Series started in the NL city on Thursday, October 1; since Sunday games were still illegal in Pennsylvania because of the "blue laws" that forbid Sabbath toil, this Series would have an added off day to the two allowed for travel after the second and fifth games. So if the Series went to seven games, Mack could start his aces, Lefty Grove and George Earnshaw, three times each, another perceived advantage for the defending champs. Each pitcher had won two games in the previous year's win over the Cardinals.

Knocking off the two-time defending champs would not be easy, and Cardinals manager Gabby Street knew it. Although known more for his optimistic outlook and his feisty defense of his players than for his tactical acumen, Street's strategy in this Series brought the title back to St. Louis. "I don't know how much hittin' we'll get off Grove and Earnshaw," he said, "so we better not waste any time on the bases. Let's run." And run they did; led by Pepper Martin, the Redbirds had the A's on their heels most of the series, especially star catcher Mickey Cochrane. And Gabby's pitching moves almost all paid off in the long run.

Before the first game of the World Series, Branch Rickey, vice president and general manager of the club, gave the squad an inspiring talk on the theme: "The greatest attribute of a winning ballplayer is a desire to win that dominates." Martin later remembered that the speech "brought every single Cardinal off his seat. . . . We rushed out of there cheering, and I personally got down on my knees in front of the dugout and kissed the ground."

Unwilling to match one of his veteran aces against the seemingly invincible Grove, Cardinals manager Gabby Street tapped rookie Paul Derringer to start the 1931 Series opener. A rangy right-handed fastballer out of Kentucky, Derringer would finish his career with 223 NL wins and would pitch the Reds to the 1940 World Championship with a 2–1 win in Game 7. But in 1931 he was not quite ready to star on the big stage. For two innings it seemed that the Birds might get lucky. Although Grove fanned two men in the first inning, three singles and a two-out double by Martin gave the home fans a two-run lead to cheer about. In the third inning, the first two A's got hits against Derringer. A strikeout and a fielder's choice nearly got him out of the jam, but a Mule Haas double drove home one run, two walks forced home another, and Jimmie Foxx's two-run single up the middle made it a four-run inning.

The Cardinals showed their aggressive style in the sixth inning, when Chick Hafey stole third base on a close play. While Philadelphia third baseman Jimmie Dykes was arguing the call, Martin stole second. But the runners were left stranded. In the next inning, Simmons poled a two-run homer. St. Louis peppered Grove for twelve hits (including three by Martin) but could not come up with any more RBI hits and lost, 6–2.

In Game 2, Hallahan walked seven while the Cardinals managed only six hits off Earnshaw. But St. Louis won 2–0, and the Legend of Pepper Martin, "The Wild Horse of the Osage," began to take hold. With one gone in the second inning, Martin lined one over the third baseman's head and raced around to second base when the left fielder slipped fielding the hit. With all eyes on him, he stole third with some help from a poor throw by catcher Mickey Cochrane. Martin came home following a long fly out by Wilson. In the seventh inning he was at it again, leading off with a single and promptly stealing second. Wilson got him to third with a grounder to the right side, then Pepper slid home safely after a neat squeeze bunt by Gelbert.

Hallahan retired the first eleven Athletics hitters, but he was constantly in trouble after that. In the fifth, a walk, a hit, and a sacrifice put men on second and third with one gone. Manager Street ordered an intentional pass to the eighth-place hitter, and then Earnshaw obliged by bouncing into a double play. In the top of the seventh, with the score still 1–0, Mack let Earnshaw bat in a crucial situation again. This time he struck out with men on first and third.

Hallahan's effort nearly came to crashing ruin in the ninth, however. He walked Foxx and Dykes but had two outs and two strikes when pinch-hitter Jimmy Moore swung and missed at a curve in the dirt. Wilson scooped up the pitch and, to the astonishment of all, threw it to third baseman Jake Flowers. Thinking the game was over, most of the Cardinals players headed for the dugout. But A's coach Eddie Collins got his men moving, and Foxx made it to third before Flowers realized just what was happening. Moore made a belated break from the batter's box and was declared safe at first on the missed third strike, loading the bases. But Wild Bill was up to the challenge, getting Max Bishop to raise a high foul near the box seats, where Bottomley made an acrobatic catch to finally seal the victory.

Hallahan, reminiscing years later with baseball writer Donald Honig, said he never understood why Wilson threw the ball to Flowers. And Hallahan said Flowers told him his instinct was to celebrate by throwing the ball into the stands. "Then Jake said he thought that maybe I would want that ball as a memento. Memento heck; I needed that ball back to get the next man out with," Hallahan recalled.

The catch by Bottomley to end the game was no easy feat, Hallahan explained, because the Cardinals first baseman had to reach into the stands. "I always said it was a lucky thing we were playing at home, because the fans got out of the way and let Jim make the play. If we had been playing in Philadelphia I'm sure they wouldn't have been so helpful."

President Herbert Hoover was on hand when play resumed for the third game, on Monday in Philadelphia. Grove started for the home team against Burleigh Grimes for the visiting Cardinals. Old "Boily," a mimicry of the pronunciation of his first name as well as a reflection of his volatile temper, hadn't pitched in a league game since September 18. Though he had had a five-inning tune-up in an exhibition on September 24, he had been laid up for a week with an appendicitis attack. At least he was well rested for this start and was, by his own admission, eager to avenge his two defeats in the 1930 Series. He breezed through the powerful Philadelphia lineup for seven innings, allowing no hits while walking only two, and getting a double play to erase one of those runners. His teammates, in the meantime, took it to Grove, scoring two in the second and two more in the fourth. Pepper Martin's hitting and running were big parts of both rallies, and even the Philadelphia crowd applauded him. Grimes himself capped off the second uprising by placing a two-out, two-run single to right field.

And when Grimes went to the hill in the bottom of the eighth, the hometown A's fans were rooting for a no-hitter. After a leadoff walk to Foxx, Grimes gave a line single to center by Bing Miller to break up the no-hit gem. But he got the next three hitters out. After his teammates added a run in the top of the ninth, Grimes retired the first two men in the bottom of the ninth before walking Cochrane. Simmons then blasted one over the fence in right field to spoil the shutout. But Grimes struck Foxx out to finish with a two-hit, 5–2 win, putting St. Louis ahead, two games to one.

The Athletics tied the series behind Earnshaw in Game 4, winning 3–0. Syl Johnson started for St. Louis, pitching credibly but taking the loss. The A's jumped out to a 1–0 lead in the first on a leadoff single by Bishop and a two-out double by Simmons. Johnson blanked them for the next three innings and retired the first two batters in the sixth. Then Jimmie Foxx unloaded with a majestic home run over the double-decked left-field stands. Earnshaw dominated the Cardinals lineup, walking one and allowing only two hits. Both singles came off the bat of Pepper Martin, who continued to earn the applause of the Philly fans.

Hallahan once again throttled the Athletics in Game 5, winning 5–1. In contrast to his three-hit, seven-walk performance in the second game, this time around he gave up nine hits but only one base on balls. Two of the safe hits were comebackers that ricocheted off Hallahan's body, but once again he was able to pitch out of trouble repeatedly.

Wild Bill's heroics notwithstanding, the day belonged to Pepper. With cleanup hitter Jim Bottomley having managed just one outfield hit through the first four games, Street flip-flopped him with Martin in the batting order, Pepper hitting fourth and Sunny Jim dropping to sixth. The move paid quick dividends in the top of the first when Martin delivered a long run-scoring flyball with one out. Pepper's game was still speed, of course, and he showed that with a bunt single in his next at-bat. But after Frisch doubled in the sixth inning, Martin muscled up and socked a home run into the upper deck in left field, upping the Cardinal lead to 3–0. After the A's had plated their only run in the bottom of the seventh, Martin got the run back with a two-out, run-scoring single to left. Trying to steal his fifth base of the series, Pepper was finally thrown out. But his ledger for the day showed three hits and four runs batted in, bringing his Series batting average to a neat .667 with twelve hits (including four doubles and a homer), five runs scored, and five more batted in.

Now it seemed that the whole world wanted to know just who was this Pepper Martin. John Leonard Martin came out of Oklahoma City with few of the inhibitions that affect most of society.

In 1925 Blake Harper, owner of the Cardinals' Fort Smith farm, nicknamed him Pepper, short for Pepperpot. Even though he left a wife and child at home, Pepper hoboed his way to spring training in 1931, riding the freights and dodging the railroad detectives. For the 1940 *Sporting News Baseball Register*, he listed his hobbies as "hunting, woodworking, machinery, managing professional boxers, and playing guitar." He was an inveterate practical joker, and for the next decade his pranks—water balloons, sneezing powder, and exploding cigars—rocked just about every hotel around the National League circuit. And he could run like the wind. A 1929 minor-league teammate started the yarn that he used to chase rabbits, picking them up and testing them for size before deciding whether to keep them for supper or let them go.

So, as the teams traveled west on Thursday, crowds gathered on the railroad platforms along the way hoping for a glimpse of baseball's sudden star, Pepper Martin. He was happy to oblige with a wave and sometimes a few words. But the adulation awed the normally rollicking Redbird. "Say, Gabby, ain't I the same guy I always was?" he plaintively asked his manager. Needing only one hit to set a World Series record, Martin began overswinging and went hitless in the final two games of the Series, although he did contribute with his speed.

With a chance to wrap up the title in Game 6, the Cardinals fell hard, losing 8–1. Lefty Grove was back in form for the A's, while Derringer again failed in the pinches. Having walked in one run in Game 1, this time the Cardinal rookie forced home two runs as part of the four-run Athletics fifth. Philadelphia got another four on the board against reliever Jim Lindsay in the seventh inning, all the runs scoring with two outs, and the last two coming in when Chick Hafey dropped a fly ball in left field. Even worse, Hafey hurt his finger on the play and would miss Game 7.

St. Louis had been primed to celebrate before Friday's game. Suddenly facing a Game 7 on Saturday, the city was gripped by anxiety. The Cardinals would be facing Earnshaw, who had pitched a two-hit shutout four days before. In this and the previous World Series, he had held the Birds to just four runs and twenty-one hits in forty-two innings, never giving up more than one run in any frame. Although the game was played on Saturday—the only weekend game of the Series—the crowd was a paltry 20,805, barely half the Friday crowd. In those days World Series tickets were sold in three-game strips, meaning that fans had to purchase tickets to three games to be assured of a seat. But Game 7 was not included in the strip sales, so everyone who wanted to attend the decisive game had to line up at the ticket window. Apparently, many expected a crush at the gates, and others dreaded the thought of watching the Cards be humbled by Earnshaw.

Those who came out, however, showed vociferous support and quickly had something to cheer about. After the A's were retired in order in the top of the first, the Cardinals turned a little luck into a pair of runs in the bottom of the round. Andy High led off with a pop fly over shortstop Dib Williams that fell safely when both left fielder Simmons and Williams pulled up to avoid a collision. On the next pitch, left-handed-hitting George Watkins hit one off the handle, but it too floated just beyond the reach of Simmons and Williams and dropped safely near the left-field line. Frisch expertly sacrificed the runners into scoring position for Martin. Earnshaw got the overeager Redbird to foul an outside pitch then missed with ball one. A vicious swing produced strike two, followed by a second ball. The next pitch was wild and behind the batter, but it hit the bat for a foul. After another foul, Earnshaw sailed one so high that Cochrane could not flag it down. High hustled home on the wild pitch while Watkins trotted to third. Ball four was next, putting Martin on first.

He did not stay there long, however, setting sail for second on the very first pitch to Ernie Orsatti. Cochrane made a strong throw, but Martin's signature belly-flop slide beat the play. Two pitches later, Orsatti chased a low one for strike three, but Cochrane dropped the ball, and Orsatti took off for first. Cochrane had to throw him out, and when he released his peg, Watkins on third broke for home. First baseman Foxx made the putout at first, but his return throw home was low and Cochrane couldn't come up with it as Watkins slid home with the second run of the round.

High and Watkins started another rally in the third; this time they couldn't be called lucky. High opened with a solid single past the diving second baseman. Watkins picked on the next pitch, a fastball that Earnshaw didn't get high enough, and drove it onto the pavilion roof for a two-run homer. Andy and Watty had now combined for four hits and four runs against Earnshaw, but that would be all the Redbirds got. The big right-hander proceeded to retire the next fifteen Cardinal batters before leaving for a pinch-hitter. It was up to Old Stubblebeard Grimes to hold the lead.

Grimes had been given an extra day of rest (and an extra day to grow his stubble), and the thirty-eight-year-old pitched the game of his life. Although the spitball was his signature pitch, the crafty right-hander also used fastballs, curves, and changeups to great effect. Two hits in the second inning and two more in the fifth gave the Mackmen some hope, but quick infield play kept the rallies from developing into runs. In the seventh, Grimes struck out the sluggers Simmons and Foxx back-to-back, yielded a hit, and then came back to fan Jimmie Dykes. That effort seemed to take something out of his arm. He labored through the eighth inning, working very slowly while walking two. He snatched a sharp comebacker to finally end the inning, keeping the score 4–0.

Grimes was a little too careful pitching to Simmons to open the ninth, walking him on a full count. Foxx, however, was retired on a foul pop, and Bing Miller smacked a double-play ball to short. Frisch flashed across the bag for the force out and gunned the ball to Bottomley at first for the apparent third out as the crowd erupted. But umpire Bill McGowan had called Miller safe. Grimes slammed his glove to the ground and rushed over to scream at the ump. But there was still one out to go, and Burleigh could not will his weary body to finish. Dykes walked, and Williams worked the count to three and two before hitting a chopper that High could not haul down. Gelbert kept the ball in the infield, but the bases were now loaded.

Hallahan had been warming up since the last inning, but Street still let Grimes stay in. Finally, after pinch-hitter Roger Cramer blooped a single to center to score two runs, Burleigh was through. Legendary sportswriter Grantland Rice lauded his effort. "He pitched his arm off and his heart out." He came up one out short. "Yet, in a way," Rice continued, "he had proved his greatness in his last-moment retreat. He had proved beyond all doubt that he had used up every ounce of his energy . . . until the moment came when he had nothing left."

Hallahan came in with a 4–2 lead and men on first and second as the crowd buzzed nervously. After all, these Athletics had clinched the 1929 Series with a three-run bottom of the ninth. Max "Camera Eye" Bishop worked the count full, and the runners took off with the next pitch. Bishop hit it hard, a high liner to left-center. But Pepper Martin had it in his sights and hauled it down. The crowd let out a roar and poured onto the field. The weary veil lifted from Grimes's shoulders, and he was one of the first to reach the mound and pound Hallahan on the back. A raucous clubhouse celebration followed, and the city partied far into the night.

In 1932, the Cardinals machine fell completely apart. The defending champions finished just 72–82, tied for sixth place. Martin slumped dismally, hitting just .238. Grimes was traded to Chicago, where he was just 6–11. Frisch played in only 115 games and hit under .300 for the first time in 12 years. But there were signs of hope as rookie Dizzy Dean won twenty games and late-season call-up Joe Medwick showed a murderous bat.

1931 Line Scores

Game 1, Thursday, October 1, at Sportsman's Park, St. Louis

	1	2	3	4	5	6	7	8	9	R	H	E
Philadelphia	0	0	4	0	0	0	2	0	0	6	11	0
St. Louis	2	0	0	0	0	0	0	0	0	2	12	0

W—Grove L—Derringer
Time—1:55 Attendance—38,529

Summary: After the Cardinals jumped out to a quick lead against Lefty Grove, the Athletics rallied for four two-out runs in the third against rookie Paul Derringer, Jimmie Foxx's two-run single breaking a tie. Al Simmons added a two-run homer in the seventh.

Game 2, Friday, October 2, at Sportsman's Park

	1	2	3	4	5	6	7	8	9	R	H	E
Philadelphia	0	0	0	0	0	0	0	0	0	0	3	0
St. Louis	0	1	0	0	0	0	1	0	x	2	6	1

W—Hallahan L—Earnshaw
Time—1:49 Attendance—35,947

Summary: Wild Bill Hallahan blanked Philadelphia despite seven walks. Pepper Martin scored both St. Louis runs, each time after stealing a base.

Game 3, Monday, October 5, at Shibe Park, Philadelphia

	1	2	3	4	5	6	7	8	9	R	H	E
St. Louis	0	2	0	2	0	0	0	0	1	5	12	0
Philadelphia	0	0	0	0	0	0	0	0	2	2	2	0

W—Grimes L—Grove
Time—2:10 Attendance—32,295

Summary: Burleigh Grimes took a no-hitter into the eighth inning and did not lose his shutout until a two-out, two-run homer in the bottom of the ninth. Martin again starred, getting key hits in the rallies in the second and fourth innings, while Grimes helped himself with a two-run single in the fourth.

Game 4, Tuesday, October 6, at Shibe Park

	1	2	3	4	5	6	7	8	9	R	H	E
St. Louis	0	0	0	0	0	0	0	0	0	0	2	1
Philadelphia	1	0	0	0	0	2	0	0	x	3	10	0

W—Earnshaw L—Johnson
Time—1:58 Attendance—32,295

Summary: George Earnshaw handcuffed the Cardinals, allowing only two hits (both by Martin). Simmons's RBI double in the first gave the A's the lead, though Foxx's mammoth home run was the biggest hit against Cardinals loser Syl Johnson.

Game 5, Wednesday, October 7, at Shibe Park

	1 2 3 4 5 6 7 8 9	R H E
St. Louis	1 0 0 0 0 2 0 1 1	5 12 0
Philadelphia	0 0 0 0 0 0 1 0 0	1 9 0

W—Hallahan L—Hoyt
Time—1:56 Attendance—32,295

Summary: Hallahan walked only one this time while pitching the Cards to an easy victory. Martin was moved into the cleanup spot and responded with four RBIs, including the go-ahead run-scoring flyball and a two-run home run.

Game 6, Friday, October 9, at Sportsman's Park

	1 2 3 4 5 6 7 8 9	R H E
Philadelphia	0 0 0 0 4 0 4 0 0	8 8 1
St. Louis	0 0 0 0 0 1 0 0 0	1 5 2

W—Grove L—Derringer
Time—1:57 Attendance—39,401

Summary: With a chance to clinch the title at home, the Redbirds played their worst game of the Series. Sloppy fielding and two bases-loaded walks gave the A's four runs in the fourth, allowing Lefty Grove to cruise to an easy victory.

Game 7, Saturday, October 10, at Sportsman's Park

	1 2 3 4 5 6 7 8 9	R H E
Philadelphia	0 0 0 0 0 0 0 0 2	2 7 1
St. Louis	2 0 2 0 0 0 0 0 x	4 5 0

W—Grimes L—Earnshaw
Time—1:57 Attendance—20,805

Summary: With Grimes out-pitching Earnshaw, St. Louis wrapped up the championship. Two pop-fly singles and daring base-running plated a pair of runs in the first, and George Watkins's home run brought home two more in the third. Grimes ran out of gas with two down in the ninth, but Hallahan got Max Bishop to line out to center with two men on for the final out.

Total attendance: 231,567
Total gate receipts: $1,030,723
Cardinals player's share: $4,467.59

1934

Cardinals Defeat Tigers 4 Games to 3

GAME 1:	**CARDINALS**	**8**	**TIGERS**	**3**
GAME 2:	**CARDINALS**	**2**	**TIGERS**	**3**
GAME 3:	**CARDINALS**	**4**	**TIGERS**	**1**
GAME 4:	**CARDINALS**	**4**	**TIGERS**	**10**
GAME 5:	**CARDINALS**	**1**	**TIGERS**	**3**
GAME 6:	**CARDINALS**	**4**	**TIGERS**	**3**
GAME 7:	**CARDINALS**	**11**	**TIGERS**	**0**

REGULAR-SEASON STARTING LINEUP		
Pepper Martin	3b	NL-leading 23 steals
Jack Rothrock	rf	NL-leading 647 at-bats
Frank Frisch	2b	.305 player/manager
Joe Medwick	lf	NL-leading 18 triples
Rip Collins	1b	.333, NL-leading 35 HRs
Spud Davis	c	.300
Ernie Orsatti	cf	.300
Leo Durocher	ss	.260, fielding specialist

PITCHERS		
Dizzy Dean	30-7	NL MVP
Paul Dean	19-11	3.43 ERA as rookie
Tex Carleton	16-11	241 innings
Bill Walker	12-4	won 8 of last 9
Bill Hallahan	8-12	won final 4 starts
Jesse Haines	4-4	now had 194 career wins
Dazzy Vance	1-1	acquired on waiver in June

BENCH	
Burgess Whitehead	inf
Chuck Fullis	of
Bill DeLancey	c

How the Cardinals Got to the World Series:

Showing the franchise's trademark late-season surge in pennant-winning years, the 1934 Cardinals wiped out a seven-game deficit in September and finished first with a 95–58 record, two games ahead of the New York Giants. Like Rogers Hornsby eight years before and Gabby Street four years previously, second baseman Frank Frisch led the Cardinals to the pennant in his first full season of managing.

The Cardinals' Series Opponent:

The Detroit Tigers won their first pennant in a quarter century, sprinting away from the New York Yankees with a 41–16 record over the last two months to win the pennant by seven games. First-year manager Mickey Cochrane, who also played 129 games and hit .320, was successful in his first year as Bengals pilot following many years as the Philadelphia A's backstop and Cardinals' opponent in the 1930 and 1931 World Series. The Tigers' offense depended on veteran left fielder Goose Goslin, hard-hitting second baseman Charlie "The Mechanical Man" Gehringer, and young slugging first baseman Hank Greenberg, who all topped .300 in batting while attaining double figures in homers and triple figures in RBIs. Right-handers Lynwood "Schoolboy" Rowe and Tommy Bridges each topped the twenty-win mark.

Getting the Tiger by the Tail

With their gray road uniforms still dirty from yesterday's game, they looked to one New York sportswriter like a bunch from Manhattan's rough Gashouse District. The "Gashouse Gang" is how we remember those wonderful 1934 World Champion St. Louis Cardinals, though it wasn't until the next year that the nickname would formally be bestowed.

"They were the best team I ever had," recalled Branch Rickey, the club's general manager. Rickey had signed most of them to their first contracts. He'd seen them develop in the farm system of minor league teams that he and Cardinals owner Sam Breadon had bought in the 1920s. Then Rickey and Breadon fought with those talented players every year over the amount they'd be paid.

"The 1934 Gashouse Gang was a high-class team, with nine heavy drinkers who were paid more money over a period of years than any other club in the National League," said Rickey, the teetotaling, penny-pinching baseball mastermind. Several Cardinals from that era would dispute the notion that their pay was among the highest in baseball. A New York sportswriter at the time stated that a coach on a Gotham team probably earned more than a star on a St. Louis club. Those 1934 Cardinals salaries ranged from $3,000 for rookie Paul Dean, $5,000 for slugging outfielder Joe Medwick, $7,500 for pitching ace Dizzy Dean, $8,000 for league home run champ Rip Collins, $9,000 for third baseman Pepper Martin, to $18,000 for manager-second baseman Frankie Frisch. Rickey earned $51,470 that year, which included 10 percent of the price the Cardinals received from the sale of any player to another team. Babe Ruth remained the highest-paid ballplayer in the land at $35,000, though he had to take a $17,000 cut during the throes of the Depression, when one of every five men was out of work.

In addition to battling the front office over pay, the Gashouse Gang fought their National League opponents—and sometimes each other. While they functioned well on the field, some personalities clashed off it. Dizzy would ride his own teammates if he felt they had let him down, and sometimes they retaliated by throwing a punch.

But that band of swashbuckling Cardinals also had lots of fun. With Pepper Martin often the ringleader, they'd give each other hot foots in the dugout or spread sneezing powder in a hotel lobby and snicker at the guests' reaction. Once, Martin, Dizzy Dean, and a few others—dressed in the white overalls of professional painters—interrupted a convention luncheon speaker to say that they were there to work but that the speaker could go on. Martin once dropped a water balloon from a balcony several stories above street level that just missed Frisch as he came out of the hotel, then rushed downstairs and feigned ignorance as he met his flummoxed manager, going back in to find the culprit.

During one particularly torrid summer day, several players wrapped themselves in blankets in the dugout while Dizzy started a bonfire in front of it. Martin, outfielder Jack Rothrock, Collins, and outfielder Ernie Orsatti would often entertain fans before the game with a sleight-of-hand ball toss among themselves. Despite his disapproval of their actions—particularly their boozing—Rickey regularly fed reporters stories about the players, helping to fuel the legend of the Gashouse Gang.

After two mediocre years since winning the 1931 World Series, the Cardinals were given little chance of winning the NL pennant by a vote of baseball scribes before the 1934 campaign began. The defending champion New York Giants were expected by most to repeat. Giants manager and first baseman Bill Terry was so confident that he dissed the crosstown rival Brooklyn Dodgers when asked how they would fare. "Brooklyn—are they still in the league?" he responded.

He'd later eat those words.

Dizzy Dean, the Cardinals' ever-colorful and never-humble pitching ace, would utter a lot of boasts and taunts—before, during, and after the season. Fortunately for him and the Cardinals, he'd fulfill his own proverb—"It ain't braggin' if you can back it up." Dizzy, only twenty-three yet a twenty-game winner the previous season, predicted that he and brother Paul, twenty-one and never the braggart, would win forty-five games for the 1934 Cardinals. For once, Dizzy understated their greatness, as the pair won forty-nine, thirty by Dizzy. Yet nine games into the season it hardly looked that way. On April 28, both Dizzy and Paul were hammered by the Chicago Cubs in a 7–1 Cardinals loss in Wrigley Field. The Cardinals were 2–7, in seventh place, and Dizzy was 1–2 with a 6.60 ERA while Paul had no decisions and a 12.00 ERA. "The only thing those Deans are good for is picking cotton, and you can print that," Cubs pitcher Guy Bush told a newspaperman.

The Cardinals promptly got back on track, winning twelve of thirteen, with the Dean brothers each notching two victories. For nine days at the end of May and beginning of June, St. Louis held first place or was tied for it before slipping back. The Redbirds would drop back to seven lengths behind a day after Labor Day. But this was no ordinary pennant race. The Deans would stage not just one but two strikes over their salaries, in June and August. The second, which included ripping up their uniforms for photographers, would result in a week's suspension—and a thirty-six-dollar bill from the team to replace the destroyed flannels. It would irritate their teammates yet galvanize them during the week's suspension as the Cardinals won five of seven games to keep pace with the Giants. Down by seven games with twenty-three to go, the Redbirds turned it up a notch.

Frisch, the grizzled veteran once known as the "Fordham Flash" for his college education at the Jesuit university and his speed, took credit for firing up his troops for the stretch drive during an impassioned clubhouse meeting before a game in Brooklyn. "'Are you fellows going to quit?'" Frisch recalled in later years of what he said to his team. "'It ain't over. If you fight to the finish, we won't be beaten.' The change was remarkable. They started kicking the benches. They dressed with fire in their eyes."

In truth, while the players followed Frisch's direction, many of them thought him lacking a necessity for a manager—the ability to think ahead. His pitchers also thought that Frisch, who called their pitches from his second-base position, wanted them to throw too many curveballs.

After Frisch's pep talk, the club won fourteen of nineteen. One game behind with four to go, the Cardinals swept a final weekend series in Sportsman's Park from the Cincinnati Reds—who fielded several former Cardinals who had helped the club win the 1926 and 1931 World Series. Dizzy won Friday's game 4–0 for his twenty-ninth win of the season. Paul also went the distance the next day, beating the Reds 6–1. Then Dizzy, on one day's rest, came back to pitch another complete-game whitewashing, 9–0. The Brooklyn Dodgers that weekend let the Giants know they indeed were still in the league by thumping New York twice, thus allowing the Cardinals to win the pennant by two lengths.

The 1934 World Series opened Wednesday, October 3, in Detroit's Navin Field, named for then-Tigers owner Frank Navin. It had been called Bennett Field until it was rebuilt in 1912, would carry the name Briggs Stadium after a new owner revamped it in 1937, and later be called Tiger Stadium until its closing following the 1999 season.

Unlike the Cardinals, who didn't clinch the pennant until the season's final day, the Tigers entered the Series well rested, having clinched six days before the regular season ended. However, that had been a mere formality since Detroit had beaten back one last bid by the Yankees in mid-September.

The Tigers were managed by Gordon "Mickey" Cochrane, the Tigers' catcher-manager, well known to the Cardinals from their battles with him when he had played for the A's against them in the 1930 and 1931 World Series. In a meaningless season-ending doubleheader against the St. Louis Browns, Cochrane had given a few innings each to his fine pitching staff: youthful twenty-game winners Lynwood Rowe and Tommy Bridges, as well as veterans Alvin Crowder, Fred Marberry, Elon Hogsett, and young Eldon Auker. Cochrane had intended to use Rowe as the first-game starter; instead, he chose experience with Crowder, known as "General" both from having served with the U.S. Army during World War I and because his last name was the same as that of General Enoch Crowder. A three-time twenty-game winner then beginning the down side of his career, Crowder had come to the Tigers in a midseason deal and gone 5–1.

Despite having better-rested pitchers such as Tex Carleton, Bill Hallahan, and Bill Walker, Frisch stuck with the man who'd brought the team home in first place: Dizzy Dean. Dizzy had purposely given newspaper reporters "scoops" about his personal life when he had come up from the minors at the end of the 1930 season. He told some his name was Jay Hanna Dean, which it was, since he'd been named for two infamous Wall Street financiers. But he told others it was Jerome Herman Dean since he'd taken the name of a boyhood friend who had died to make the boy's father happy. Dean noted for some that he had been born in January, for others August, or still others October until the team clarified that it had been January 16, 1910, in Lucas, Arkansas. Different versions of how he got the nickname "Dizzy" exist, all tied to colorful exploits before he got to the majors.

What was never disputed was that he was one hell of pitcher, a workhorse with tremendous stamina, willpower, and above all confidence. He pitched 280 innings in his 33 starts in 1934—almost Herculean by today's standards. But he had also hurled thirty-one innings in seventeen relief appearances, in an era when starters often came out of the pen when needed.

Dean caused a stir by walking over to the Tigers' bullpen to watch Crowder warm up, taunting both him and Cochrane before they angrily told him to scram, then went by the Tigers' dugout and snatched one of their bats, telling them, "You guys don't know what bats are for anyway."

Teammate Durocher said, "There was never anything vicious about Diz," which is perhaps one reason he got away with his razzing. Durocher added that while Diz took credit for what he did, he acknowledged the contributions of his teammates. "He'd be around patting everyone on the back, saying, 'That's the way to hit, Joe (Medwick) . . . that's the way to get me runs, Pepper.'"

Dean then horsed around with Al Schacht, "the Clown Prince of Baseball," who donned a tiger outfit and acted as if he were devouring the Cardinals right-hander. Paul Dean, watching his brother warm up, later said that what was supposed to be Dizzy's curve came in "as straight as the foul line."

Dean wasn't his sharpest, giving up eight hits and three runs while walking a couple. But the Tigers' defense was most obliging, making five errors. Two of them—a boot by second baseman Charley Gehringer and a bad throw by third baseman Marv Owen, allowed the Cardinals to load the bases with two outs in the second. Jack Rothrock then singled home two runs to give the Redbirds the lead they never relinquished.

Two more Detroit miscues gave the Cardinals another run in the third, one a wild throw by shortstop Billy Rogell trying to complete a double play, and one on a ground ball off the bat of

Cardinals catcher Bill DeLancey that went under the glove of Hank Greenberg, the Tigers' slugging first baseman.

After the Tigers clawed for a run in their half of that inning, Medwick muscled one over the left-field fence for a solo homer in the fifth. Medwick preferred the nickname "Muscles" and hated the "Ducky" he was saddled with after a female fan said he walked like a "ducky wucky." Then showing they could score without any help from Detroit's defense, the Cardinals plated three more in the sixth off reliever Fred Marberry.

By the time Dean surrendered a long solo home run to Greenberg in the home half of the eighth, the Cardinals had the first game well in hand.

Some newsmen noted in their game accounts that the Tigers had seemed uptight, the Cardinals free as, well, birds. Dizzy, with his usual lack of modesty, after the game said, "Them Tigers wasn't as good as I figured they belonged to be."

Having held Rowe, his ace, for fear of having him go up against Dizzy Dean, Cochrane now had to use him against veteran Bill Hallahan in Game 2. Lynwood Rowe was nicknamed "Schoolboy" because as a teenager he'd pitched on a men's team. The six-foot-four-inch right-hander had potential but not much ambition until Cochrane straightened him out, *Sporting News* editor J. G. Taylor Spink wrote in his pre-Series report: "Cochrane changed Rowe from a pitcher with a variety of deliveries to a well-controlled straight overhand hurler with terrific speed, a grand change of pace and a baffling curve." It had allowed Rowe to go 24–8 with a 3.45 ERA over 266 innings.

The Cardinals didn't seem fazed by any of Rowe's pitches in the early part of the game. Orsatti boomed a triple to score DeLancey from first with one out in the second for 1–0 lead. Medwick, after looking at strike three to end the first, smacked a pitch into left to score Martin from second with two out in the fourth to up the lead to 2–0. However, Medwick ran the Cardinals out of the inning—

and perhaps the ball game—when he tried to score on Collins's single to left and was thrown out at the plate.

Rowe would retire the next twenty-two Cardinals batters.

But Hallahan, while giving up six hits and four walks, pitched out of his jams and kept the Tigers at bay. He gave up a run in the fourth on a two-out single by Pete Fox, the Tigers' right fielder who batted eighth. Going into the bottom of the ninth, though, Wild Bill held a 2–1 lead.

Fox led off with a single and was sacrificed into scoring position by Rowe, a show of managerial confidence in a pitcher in that situation not often seen today. Gerald Walker then pinch-hit for center fielder Jo-Jo White and appeared to produce the second out when he popped a foul between home and first. A strong cross-field wind had made judging fly balls difficult all day and made it so for both Collins and DeLancey as the ball fell untouched despite Collins's valiant attempt. Given a second chance, Walker singled in the tying run.

Rowe continued to mow down the Redbirds in extra innings, pitching around a one-out double by Martin in the eleventh. In the home half of the twelfth, Cardinals reliever Bill Walker issued bases on balls to Gehringer and Greenberg with one out. Goose Goslin, another veteran Navin had picked up for the 1934 campaign, then evened the Series by singling up the middle. The twelve-inning affair—broadcast nationally through a $100,000 sponsorship from Henry Ford—had required only 2:49. More than 43,000 filled the park, about 1,000 more than the day before.

Rowe's pitching performance was all the more remarkable considering that the Cardinals bench rode him all game. In a radio interview before the Series, Rowe had bashfully asked his fiancée on air, "How'm I doin', Edna?" which became a favorite retort of the Cardinals bench jockeys.

Frisch, meanwhile, ordered newsmen out of the Cardinals clubhouse while he vented his anger and disappointment with his club's effort.

Since St. Louis and Detroit were within a day's train ride of each other, there was no scheduled off day for travel, and the Series' third game was at Sportsman's Park on Friday, October 5, a sunny and warm fall day. Now the other Dean, Paul, had the chance to show his stuff.

Newspaper reporters had invented the nickname "Daffy" for the younger Dean, something he disliked and which in no way describes his mental or emotional makeup. But Paul was no wallflower. While far from the braggadocio, Paul could play straight man to Dizzy's comedic outbursts—and be ready at the drop of a cap to fight with him against teammate and foe if either brother felt he'd been insulted.

With several days to work on the Sportsman's Park field, groundskeepers had it looking as good as they could, the *Globe-Democrat* reported. "Seven wagonloads of dirt had been brought in, the skinned portion as flat as a billiard table and the outfield as smooth as a lawn tennis court," the newspaper reported.

In two hours and seven minutes, despite not being at his best, Paul Dean tamed the Tigers 4–1, beating Tommy Bridges, Detroit's other twenty-game winner. Dean gave up eight hits and five walks and retired the side in order only in the seventh and eighth.

Leadoff man Pepper Martin got the scoring going in the home half of the first by turning a double to right into a triple with a daring dash and his signature head-first slide into third. The next man, Rothrock, drove him home with a long run-scoring flyball to the flagpole that sprouted from the center-field grass in front of the wall.

Paul Dean then gave himself the run needed for victory when he drove in Collins with a run-scoring flyball in the second. Dean lost his shutout in the ninth when Greenberg boomed a two-out triple, plating Jo-Jo White.

The younger Dean after the game complained that he'd had "the lousiest curveball I'd ever had in my life" and owed it to his not having pitched in six days. But buddy Martin chimed in that

Dean's fastball that day made up for it.

Game 4 would be the most controversial in the Series. Frisch went with Tex Carleton, whose sixteen wins had been overlooked by many because of the attention paid to the Dean brothers. His opponent was Eldon Auker, whose submarine-style delivery had earned him fifteen wins. But Cochrane had more ammunition for this battle—advice from Babe Ruth before the game and Cochrane's decision to move slugging first baseman Hank Greenberg back to the number-six slot in the batting order, from where he'd hit many of his twenty-six homers and produced most of his 139 RBIs. The move would pay off—big.

Detroit took advantage of an error by Martin, who it seemed often stopped as many balls with his body as with his glove, and a wild pitch in building a 4–2 lead going into the home half of the fourth. The Cardinals rallied when pinch-hitter Spud Davis singled home Orsatti and sent Leo Durocher to third with the tying run. Frisch put Dizzy Dean in as a pinch runner for Davis, which immediately electrified the crowd. However, the move was called using "a million dollar asset for a ten-cent job" by then sportswriter Paul Gallico of the *Chicago Tribune*. Martin grounded to the second baseman, whose throw to shortstop Billy Rogell forced Dean; when Rogell tried to complete a double play, his throw hit Dean, coming in standing up, in the head and caromed into right field as Durocher scored the tying run. Dean, meanwhile, lay stunned. His teammates carried him off the field. When Dean came to, he immediately asked if Pepper had been safe at first.

Bill Walker, the third Cardinals pitcher, kept it deadlocked at four until the seventh, when Greenberg got the third of his four hits and gave the Tigers the lead for good. They added five more off Walker and the now-ancient Pop Haines in the eighth to put the game away, evening the Series with a 10–4 thumping that disappointed Cardinals fans among the 37,492 watching.

Cardinals announcer France Laux, silenced during the regular season by Cardinals owner Breadon's ban on radio broadcasts but back on the national radio coverage financed by Ford, said later that Dizzy had begged Frisch to enter the game as a pinch runner. Frisch, grilled by reporters about the move later, merely said that a play like that wouldn't happen for another fifteen years. Then he noted with some humor that Dean at least had broken up the double play. And he added that Dizzy, who'd suffered what Frisch called a "minor injury," would start the fifth game. There was no headline in any newspaper the next day stating that "X-rays of Dizzy's head show nothing," though for years that was the common joke. Even Dizzy reportedly told it himself. But he was eager and ready to pitch the next day.

While the spirit was willing, Dean's pitching wasn't. He gave up six hits and three walks in his eight innings. He walked Greenberg with one out in the second then gave up an RBI double with two outs to eighth-place-hitting Pete Fox. Leading off the sixth with a home run was Tigers second baseman Charley Gehringer, whose steady play at second and RBI production seemed so automatic he was dubbed "The Mechanical Man." Later in the frame, Greenberg hit a run-scoring flyball after yet another Cardinals error, by center fielder Ernie Orsatti, had turned a single into a three-base play.

Tommy Bridges, starting on one day's rest following his four innings in Game 3, scattered seven hits and didn't walk anyone. The Cardinals never put two on base in the same inning until the ninth and scored their only run on a homer by catcher Bill DeLancey in the seventh. Cochrane was ecstatic. "We have the Cardinals on the run, and I'm anxious to get it over with," he said as the team prepared to return to Detroit for Game 6 the next day.

Meanwhile, the St. Louis Convention, Publicity and Tourism Bureau happily reported that approximately 15,000 World Series visitors had boosted the St. Louis economy over the previous three days by spenting an average of twenty dollars per day per person. That broke down at ten dollars for a hotel room and the other ten dollars covering the cost of a Series ticket, a taxi ride, liquor, and food.

Frisch at first said he didn't know whom he'd choose for Game 6. But there seemed to be little choice. As Paul and Dizzy had won the last two regular-season games that had broken a first-place tie with the Giants, Paul would be counted on for Game 6 and Dizzy for a Game 7.

Jim Mooney, a fine pitcher relegated to the bullpen because of the Deans' workload, commented later on the closeness between the brothers Dean. "(Paul) believed in Dizzy, and Dizzy believed in Paul. One of them would be out there pitching, and the other would be sitting on the bench as the game was going on, and he'd say, 'Boy, there's the best pitcher in baseball.' And the next day, why the other would say the same thing about the one on the mound."

A crowd of 44,551 turned out at Navin Field hoping to see Rowe again dominate the Cardinals. But they saw the Redbirds waste no time in getting ahead. After Pepper Martin popped out to begin the game, Jack Rothrock doubled and one out later scored on a single by Medwick.

Cochrane drove in the tying run for the Tigers in the third when he topped the ball to the right side and beat Paul Dean to the bag. But Dean accidentally spiked Cochrane, who stayed in the game despite the pain.

Errors continued to play a big part of this Series. In the fifth, light-hitting shortstop Leo Durocher—whom Babe Ruth once called "The All-American Out"—led off with a single, was sacrificed to second by Dean, then scored on Martin's single to left. Martin went to third on the left fielder's throwing error to the plate and scored on a ground out.

But the Tigers tied the contest the next inning. Jo-Jo White led off with a walk and moved to third on Cochrane's single. When Dean bobbled Gehringer's grounder, White scored and Cochrane moved to second. He scored the tying run two outs later on a hit by Greenberg, thoroughly making the best of his return to the sixth spot in the order.

A pitcher who can help himself at the plate has an edge. When Durocher doubled with one out in the seventh, Dean promptly followed with a single to right driving him home and giving the Cardinals a 4–3 lead.

The pesky Fox led off the home seventh with a double, and Cochrane again stuck with Rowe, having him sacrifice the tying run to third. But Durocher, complementing his hitting, threw Fox out at home on a ground ball by Jo-Jo White. Then DeLancey ended the inning by gunning out White trying to steal.

Dean stranded two baserunners in the eighth then sent down the Tigers 1-2-3 in the ninth. The Series was tied. Always a sharp dresser who liked high society, Durocher sometimes had been a divisive element on the team because his fellow Gashousers thought he was too close to the team's ownership; but he now gladly accepted the congratulations of his reinvigorated teammates.

There have been many great seventh games of the World Series, nail-biters that often went down to the last out, and the Cardinals have been part of several. The 1934 finale, however, was not among them.

The Cardinals removed the drama in the third inning. Twelve batters banged out seven hits and scored seven runs off four Tigers pitchers—the cream of Cochrane's pitching staff. Dizzy Dean started it with a double and scored with Martin and Rothrock when Frisch cleared the bases with a double. The blow caused Cochrane to yank Eldon Auker and bring back the previous day's starter, Rowe. He surrendered RBI hits to Collins—who so loved the nickname "Rip" that he included it in his telephone book listing—and DeLancey before surrendering the mound to Elon Hogsett. He gave up an infield single to Dean that drove in the sixth run, then walked Martin with the bases loaded. Tommy Bridges came out of the bullpen to retire Rothrock to end the inning.

Back on the mound, Diz was Ol' Diz: Though pitching again on only one day's rest he didn't allow a hit until the fourth, and only six safeties for the game while walking none and fanning five. The Tigers moved only one runner as far as third, and Dizzy squelched him and the other two runners that got in scoring position.

The final was 11–0. The game is remembered, if at all, because of a nasty incident involving one of the Cardinals' nastiest players: Joe Medwick. With two out in the sixth and Martin on second, Medwick belted a pitch from Tommy Bridges off the right-center-field wall and hustled all the way to third for a triple. But as Medwick slid, he spiked Marv Owen, the Tigers' third baseman, who then tumbled onto the sliding runner. The two scuffled briefly, and Owen refused Medwick's offer of a handshake.

When he went to his left-field position after the inning, Medwick was pelted by produce—apples, oranges, bananas, lemons, potatoes, and empty soda bottles—from fans already dismayed at seeing their heroes getting pasted. Medwick later said he could understand the fans' frustration but wondered why they had brought produce to the game in the first place.

The deluge delayed the game. Commissioner Kenesaw Mountain Landis, a federal judge before being hired as commissioner in 1920, then ordered Medwick out of the game while allowing Owen to continue. Medwick was incensed: He had eleven hits for the Series, one short of the record Martin had set in the 1931 Series, and now was denied the chance to tie it.

Owen was responsible for the final out of the game when he forced a runner at second, sure-handed Durocher flipping the ball to Frisch. The Cardinals needed a police escort back to the hotel, and a plainclothes detective was assigned specifically to protect Medwick for the journey home. But that didn't deter the Gashouse Gang from celebrating. They were the best team in baseball. And each of them was $5,389.57 richer through the winning players' share of the World Series receipts.

Dizzy, ever the egomaniac, in his ghost-written newspaper column the next day told Bridges to tell his grandkids that he'd once beaten the great Dean. But he also couldn't pass tipping his cap to Paul. "I was pleased to show that I could pitch about as good as that kid brother of mine," Dizzy wrote.

The Gashouse Gang returned in 1935 and appeared headed for a second straight pennant in September and another rematch with the Tigers, who again won the AL pennant easily. Paul Dean again won nineteen games and Dizzy came down just a notch, to twenty-eight. But the Chicago Cubs won twenty-one straight in September, taking over first place from the Cardinals in mid-month. The Cubs clinched the pennant at Sportsman's Park on the final Friday of the season, beating Dizzy Dean to do so.

Paul Dean would never win more than five games in any of his seven remaining seasons. A line drive off the bat of Earl Averill in the 1937 All-Star Game would break Dizzy's toe and lead him to the broadcasting booth. Frisch got old and was fired in 1938, a season which saw only Medwick still in the starting lineup from the 1934 bunch. The former champions tumbled to sixth place. But the seeds of the St. Louis Swifties, who would restore the Redbirds to glory in the 1940s, had already been sown with the addition of Enos Slaughter and Terry Moore—and a few more coming up from the ever-fertile farm system.

1934 Line Scores

Game 1, Wednesday, October 3, at Navin Field, Detroit

	1	2	3	4	5	6	7	8	9	R	H	E
St. Louis	0	2	1	0	1	4	0	0	0	8	13	2
Detroit	0	0	1	0	0	1	0	1	0	3	8	5

W—D. Dean L—Crowder
Time—2:13 Attendance—42,505

Summary: Five Detroit errors aided Cardinals offense while Dizzy Dean scattered Detroit's hits to give Cardinals opening-game win.

Game 2, Thursday, October 4, at Navin Field

	1	2	3	4	5	6	7	8	9	10	11	12	R	H	E
St. Louis	0	1	1	0	0	0	0	0	0	0	0	0	2	7	3
Detroit	0	0	0	1	0	0	0	0	1	0	0	1	3	7	0

W—Rowe L—Walker
Time—2:49 Attendance—43,451

Summary: Cardinals learned lesson from slants of Schoolboy Rowe, who retired 22 straight from third inning into the eleventh. Tigers pushed across winning run in 12th on Goose Goslin's RBI single.

Game 3, Friday, October 5, at Sportsman's Park, St. Louis

	1	2	3	4	5	6	7	8	9	R	H	E
Detroit	0	0	0	0	0	0	0	0	1	1	8	2
St. Louis	1	1	0	0	2	0	0	0	x	4	9	1

W—P. Dean L—Bridges
Time—2:07 Attendance—34,073

Summary: Paul Dean allowed 13 baserunners but only one run while Pepper Martin's running and Jack Rothrock's batting plated tallies Cardinals needed for win.

Game 4, Saturday, October 6, at Sportsman's Park

	1	2	3	4	5	6	7	8	9	R	H	E
Detroit	0	0	3	1	0	0	1	5	0	10	13	1
St. Louis	0	1	1	2	0	0	0	0	0	4	10	5

W—Auker L—Walker
Time—2:43 Attendance—37,492

Summary: Pepper Martin's three errors aided Tigers' scoring, and Detroit batters, led by Hank Greenberg's four hits, punished quintet of Cardinals pitchers to even Series. Dizzy Dean broke up double play—with his head getting in way of shortstop's throw.

Game 5, Sunday, October 7, at Sportsman's Park

	1 2 3 4 5 6 7 8 9	R	H	E
Detroit	0 1 0 0 0 2 0 0 0	3	7	0
St. Louis	0 0 0 0 0 0 1 0 0	1	7	1

W—Bridges L—D. Dean
Time—1:58 Attendance—38,536

Summary: Despite being KO'd the day before on baselines, Dizzy Dean pitched valiantly but was no match for Tigers' Tommy Bridges, aided by Greenberg's homer.

Game 6, Monday, October 8, at Navin Field

	1 2 3 4 5 6 7 8 9	R	H	E
St. Louis	1 0 0 0 2 0 1 0 0	4	10	2
Detroit	0 0 1 0 0 2 0 0 0	3	7	1

W—P. Dean L—Rowe
Time—1:58 Attendance—44,551

Summary: Paul Dean pitched and batted Cardinals to win, throttling Tigers on seven hits while driving in tiebreaker with single in seventh, thus forcing seventh game.

Game 7, Tuesday, October 9, at Navin Field

	1 2 3 4 5 6 7 8 9	R	H	E
St. Louis	0 0 7 0 0 2 2 0 0	11	17	1
Detroit	0 0 0 0 0 0 0 0 0	0	6	3

W—D. Dean L—Auker
Time—2:19 Attendance—40,902

Summary: Cardinals captured world crown by dismantling three pitchers in early seven-run outburst while Dizzy Dean tamed Tigers with whitewashing. Game was marred by trash-tossing incident by fans against Cardinals left fielder Joe Medwick after his hard slide into third baseman Marv Owen.

Total attendance: 281,510
Total gate receipts: $1,031,341
Cardinals player's share: $5,389.57

1942

Cardinals Defeat Yankees 4 Games to 1

GAME 1:	CARDINALS	4	YANKEES	7
GAME 2:	CARDINALS	4	YANKEES	3
GAME 3:	CARDINALS	2	YANKEES	0
GAME 4:	CARDINALS	9	YANKEES	6
GAME 5:	CARDINALS	4	YANKEES	2

REGULAR-SEASON STARTING LINEUP		
Jimmy Brown	2b-3b	shifted to 2b in July
Terry Moore	cf	.288, team captain
Enos Slaughter	rf	.318
Stan Musial	lf	.315 as a rookie
Walker Cooper	c	.281, All-Star
Johnny Hopp	1b	.281 down the stretch
Whitey Kurowski	3b	39 RBIs after All-Star Game
Marty Marion	ss	NL-leading 38 doubles

PITCHERS		
Mort Cooper	22-7	NL MVP
Johnny Beazley	21-6	2.13 ERA as rookie
Max Lanier	13-8	5-2 vs. Brooklyn
Harry Gumbert	9-5	19 starts, 19 relief appearances
Howie Pollet	7-5	2 shutouts in 13 starts
Howie Krist	13-3	2.51 ERA (1.70 in relief)
Ernie White	7-5	3-0 in September

BENCH	
Frank Crespi	2b
Ray Sanders	1b
Harry Walker	of
Coaker Triplett	of

How the Cardinals Got to the World Series:

The young and coming Cardinals overcame a ten-game Dodgers lead to win the pennant with a breathtaking race to the finish. Over the last fifty days of the season, St. Louis won forty-three games while losing only eight to wind up two games ahead of Brooklyn. Manager Billy Southworth's team had a 106–48 won-lost record, setting a St. Louis record for wins that still stands.

The Cardinals' Series Opponent:

The defending World Champion New York Yankees won 103 games in 1942 to breeze to their sixth pennant in seven years. The Bronx Bombers had won every World Series they had played in since losing to the Cardinals in 1926, dropping only four games in those eight Series.

Southworth's Swifties Stun the Mighty Yankees

Measured by their regular-season games won and the fact that they beat a good Yankees team for the championship, the 1942 Cardinals rate as the greatest of all St. Louis baseball teams. The club captured the National League pennant with 106 wins, establishing a franchise record that still stands, and achieved more victories than any NL team between 1909 and 1975. Even more impressive was that they beat the Yankees in five games in the World Series. The Bronx Bombers had won in all eight of their Series appearances over the previous fifteen seasons, piling up a 32–4 record in those eight Fall Classics.

Yet it was a Cardinals championship that very nearly did not happen. Although Manager Billy Southworth's Redbirds had been heavy preseason favorites to win the pennant, they fell behind the defending champion Brooklyn Dodgers by ten games in early August. The Dodgers were on a pace to win 109 games, so overtaking them seemed impossible. When Cardinals owner Sam Breadon peddled veteran pitching star Lon Warneke (the team's highest-salaried player) to the Cubs in early July for $75,000, it looked to the fans that management had written off the season. Vice President Branch Rickey later admitted, "I had given up. Who hadn't? Who but Southworth? He said all along we could still win, (and he) still had supreme courage and confidence. It was no act of duty with

Southworth, no false front. He believed in the team and he made the team believe in itself."

Down the stretch, the Cardinals were almost unbeatable, winning forty-one games while losing only seven, including five out of six head-to-head meetings with the Dodgers. A two-game sweep in Brooklyn in mid-September finally lifted St. Louis into a tie for first place with two weeks to go. The Dodgers did not collapse, winning ten of their final fourteen games. But that was not good enough to beat the surging Cardinals, who won twelve of fourteen to take the pennant by two lengths. Although Rickey had been at odds with Breadon over the hiring of Southworth, he gladly lauded the manager's work now, opining, "I know of no other example of inspirational courage like Southworth's in the history of baseball competition."

While he could be effusive in his praise of Southworth, Rickey would find the 1942 Cardinals to be a fitting valedictory for his twenty-six years with the team. His farm system was operating at peak efficiency, with all but one of the men on the active World Series roster having come up through the Cardinals organization. But this would be the end of his association with the club. His five-year contract was due to expire in December, and Breadon had informed him it would not be renewed. That contract paid Rickey a $50,000 base salary plus a percentage of the proceeds from the sale of players to other clubs. His estimated earnings for 1941 had been $88,000, making it the richest contract in the game, well above Commissioner Kenesaw Mountain Landis's $65,000 per annum.

Landis and Rickey had long been at loggerheads about the farm system, and in March 1938, the commissioner had penalized the Cardinals for contract abuses by declaring seventy-four Cardinals minor leaguers free agents. Rickey had wanted to sue Landis in civil court to reverse the ruling, but Breadon had refused to do so. In 1940, just days after Rickey had told the press that Cardinals manager Ray Blades's job was secure, Breadon had fired the skipper and hired Southworth. The move turned out to be a good one, but the rift between club president and vice president became wider.

For Breadon and all other major league owners, the future was murky at best. How would the wartime draft affect professional sports? President Franklin D. Roosevelt had already given a green light to allow baseball to continue, but minor league attendance dropped substantially in 1942. And whereas thirty minor leagues operated in 1942, only ten would start in 1943. Less overtly, Breadon, who had been a car salesman before becoming Cardinals president in 1920, wanted to show that he knew enough to operate a ball club without the supposed genius, Rickey, at his elbow. So it came as little surprise when Rickey resigned a few weeks after the 1942 World Series to become president and general manger of the Brooklyn baseball club.

The last Cardinals team assembled by Rickey was very young but very talented, and Manager Southworth earned the players' respect and devotion by his attention to their well-being—showing a much different approach than he had when managing the team for one season thirteen years before. As an outfielder he'd been one of the stars of the Cardinals' 1926 World Series win over the Yankees. But three years later as a rookie manager his hard-line attitude toward his former teammates had caused some of them to label him a "heel." After a disastrous half-season in 1929, he was demoted to minor-league managing.

In 1942, however, Southworth never chided his players in public, often deflecting criticism of them to himself. Although he was strict in enforcing his rules, he handled problems behind closed doors and not in the press. By the end of the season, the squad was policing itself. After that key September series in Brooklyn, captain Terry Moore called a meeting of the players in which they pledged that, "None of us will stay out late at night or do anything that'll keep us from being at our very best."

Moore was one of only two regulars to have reached thirty

years of age, and he looked after the younger men, getting on them gently if they made mistakes, but also lending an ear if they had problems. As a batsman he was good but not great, but as a fly-hawk he was almost beyond great. Arthur Daley of the *New York Times* called him "a wizard with a magical glove. He could make triples, doubles, and singles disappear by a mere wave of that glove. Presto, change and they reappeared as putouts."

The graybeard in the infield was Jimmy Brown, the team's lead-off hitter. A farm boy who had gone to North Carolina State College, his age was listed as thirty in 1942, though he was actually two years older. Having come up to the team in 1937, he was touched by the Gashouse Gang and described by his former manager, Frank Frisch, as "the kind of fellow who loves to win, will break his neck trying, and has no use for anybody who doesn't feel the same way he does."

Brown could cover second base, third base, or shortstop adequately, and early in the season Southworth had stationed him at third. Second baseman Frank Crespi was a good fielder, but a rookie named George "Whitey" Kurowski, better suited for third base, made enough key hits to force his way into the lineup, and Brown was shifted to second. Kurowski delivered the biggest hit of the regular season on September 12, a two-run home run in Brooklyn that beat the Bums 2–1 and finally got the Cardinals into a tie for first place.

Southworth also made a switch at first base, giving Johnny Hopp the majority of the starts in the second half of the season. While erstwhile starter Ray Sanders stood six feet two and had some long-ball potential, Hopp was a compact five feet nine and geared toward short line drives and daring running. His biggest moment came in Wrigley Field with one week to go in the season when he scored on a double steal to beat old teammate Warneke 1–0. Hopp was better suited for center field, but the 1942 Cardinals outfield was one of the greatest in history.

Left field started with a platoon of veteran Coaker Triplett, a right-handed hitter, and rookie Stan Musial, a left-handed swinger. Musial kept his average over .300, thanks in part to Triplett taking at-bats against tough lefties, and finished third in the league with a .315 mark.

Right fielder Enos Slaughter was ahead of him at .318 and would have won the batting title if current rules had been used. He did lead the league in hits, triples, and total bases. No player personified Cardinals baseball better than he did. Solidly built and fast afoot, he barreled around the bases with breakneck abandon, and infielders could get bowled over if they stood their ground. In the outfield, he had speed and a strong, accurate arm. And he always hustled, always, even running hard going to his position between innings.

Shortstop was the wide realm of Marty Marion, in his third season with the team and already rated as the top defensive player in the league. Long-limbed and lean he had both smooth movements and fantastic range. Although he usually batted eighth, Marion had some line-drive power and wound up leading the league in doubles with thirty-eight.

The team's battery work revolved around the brothers Cooper, pitcher Mort and catcher Walker. They were just coming into their own in 1942 and served as All-Star Game starters in 1942. Mort was 11–4 at the break, but his chronic elbow problems began to affect him in July and August. He adopted a regimen of chewing aspirin tablets to dull the pain. But he won only two of his first seven starts after the break, and it looked like he might get stuck at thirteen wins again, just as he had in 1941, when he had gone 0–4 in September to finish 13–9. Not that Mort was the superstitious sort; 13 was his uniform number. But when he took the mound on August 14, he was wearing No. 14. New number or whatever, Mort's magic returned, and he blanked the Reds on two hits for his fourteenth win. So every game thereafter he switched to the win number he was looking for. It worked like a charm: In his last ten starts he gave up only eleven runs, though it did take him two tries for win No. 22, while barely squeezing into Murry Dickson's diminutive shirt. His only loss in the last nine weeks came as a reliever, when he was wearing his old No. 13. He wound up leading the league in wins (22), shutouts (10), and ERA (1.77), and was named the NL's Most Valuable Player.

Rookie right-hander Johnny Beazley compiled a 21–6 record and a 2.17 earned run average.

Although the Cardinals did not clinch the pennant until the final day of the season, Southworth had Cooper well rested for the opening game of the World Series with Beazley available for Game 2 on his normal three days of rest. The "St. Louis Swifites," as the Cardinals were beginning to be called, were red hot and confident, having swept their final six-game homestand to cinch the flag. Southworth was sure his youngster would not be intimidated by the Yankees and their reputation of invincibility.

But the Bronx Bombers had made hash of every NL champ that came down the pike, and in the Series opener the 1942 Cardinals looked like just another victim. New York manager Joe McCarthy tapped old Charles "Red" Ruffing to pitch Game 1, even though he had had a modest 14–7 record. But Ruffing had been winning World Series games for McCarthy since 1932 and had won his last five Series starts, all complete games. Cooper matched zeroes with Ruffing through three innings, but key doubles by Buddy Hassett and Roy Cullenbine helped the Yanks to single runs in the fourth and fifth innings. Cardinal fans still held out some hope until the eighth, when three New York singles and a two-out, two-run error by Slaughter made the score 5–0 and knocked Cooper out of the game.

There was still drama, however. Through seven innings Ruffing had walked five men and had repeatedly growled at the home-plate umpire, George Magerkurth. But he had allowed no hits. He got the first two outs in the bottom of the eighth before Moore, usually a dead-pull right-handed hitter, lined a clean single to right field to end the no-hit bid. Slaughter got hold of one, but Joe DiMaggio ran it down in deep right center to end the inning. Southworth sent Max Lanier to pitch the ninth. The lefty had won thirteen games during the regular season, including five critical decisions against Brooklyn, and many people assumed he would start the third game against the Yankees. But in his World Series debut, he made two embarrassing errors to hand New York two more runs.

With a 7–0 lead, Ruffing got a foul pop out, yielded an infield single, then got a routine fly to move to within one out of his seventh career World Series win. But pinch-hitter Sanders worked a walk and Marion tripled into the right-field corner to break up the shutout. Two more hits followed, and McCarthy had to yank his starter and bring in Spud Chandler to close out the game. The Cardinals were still not ready to go. Two hits off of Chandler made the score 7–4 with the bases loaded. Sportsman's Park, which had been eerily quiet just minutes before, was now in an uproar. The batter was Stan Musial, who had made the first out of the inning. But fans remembered that he had hit a dramatic grand slam just eight days before. This time, however, the youngster—several years away from gaining his nickname "The Man"—hit a routine grounder to first base to end the game.

"I am sure those four runs we scored with two out in the ninth inning of the first game will serve as a tonic for my boys," Southworth said before Game 2, "and I think you'll find us a steadier team." How right he was. Right from the start it seemed that the Yankees were suddenly jittery. New York pitcher Ernie Bonham, renowned for his control, walked St. Louis leadoff man Jimmy Brown on five pitches. When Terry Moore followed with a well-deadened sacrifice attempt, Bonham made an ill-advised throw to second, and both runners were safe. Bonham settled down and retired the next two hitters. But Walker Cooper rifled a shot past second baseman Joe Gordon, who was playing near the base to hold Brown close. The ball scooted all the way to the outfield wall, and Brown and Moore raced home.

Bonham's pitching opponent was also a twenty-one-game winner: Nashville, Tennessee, native Johnny Beazley. He was devoted to the single mother who had raised him, and proudly doted on her when she came to St. Louis for the Series. She gave her son a good-luck kiss before he went out to warm up. On the mound Johnny was no mama's boy, however, balancing a hot temper with remarkable fortitude under fire. The Yankees got a runner at least as far as second base in each of the first five innings of the game, but Johnny blanked them each time. Even when he finally had a 1–2–3 inning in the sixth, two of the hitters were retired with the count full.

Bonham had no trouble getting through the next five innings, but the Birds added another run in the seventh. With one out, Johnny Hopp smacked an 0–2 pitch to right for a hit. Whitey Kurowski then lifted a drive down the left-field line. Outfielder Charlie Keller lunged for it near the line but could not make the catch. The ball appeared to land foul, but umpire George Magerkurth called it fair. The ball bounded into the corner, scoring Hopp easily and allowing Kurowski to advance to third base. The Yankees argued long and hard, but, of course, the ruling stood.

Beazley retired the first two hitters in the eighth before the New York offense came to life. Cullenbine was safe on an infield smash, stole second, and scored when DiMaggio lined a hit to right. On the very next pitch, Keller unloaded a howitzer shot onto the pavilion roof for a game-tying home run. But Beazley struck out Joe Gordon on three pitches to close the frame.

Bonham was beginning to tire, going to a full count before retiring each of the first two hitters in the bottom of the eighth. Then Slaughter pulled a fastball into the right-field corner and raced for second. When the relay deflected off of shortstop Phil Rizzuto's glove, Enos continued to third. Musial followed with his first hit of the Series, a sharp slapper up the middle, and the Cardinals were back in the lead, 4–3. But Slaughter had more work to do. In the ninth, the first two Yankees singled. But Slaughter's one-hop bullet from right gunned down pinch-runner Tuck Stainback trying to go from first to third, and Beazley retired the last two men to give the Cardinals a win to even the Series. Billy the Kid's Redbirds were exuberant after the victory, while the Yankees were left to think about the "What ifs."

After a travel day, the Series resumed in New York in front of a full house of more than 69,000 in Yankee Stadium. Southworth's choice of Ernie White raised some eyebrows, but it turned out to be a brilliant move. Backed by some great outfielding, the little South Carolina left-hander handed the mighty Yankees their first World Series shutout defeat since Jess Haines had turned the trick in 1926. White gave up six hits (but never two in the same inning) and walked no one.

With two out and one on in the sixth, DiMaggio blasted one toward the gap in left center, splitting Moore and Musial perfectly. As the pair closed on the fly, Terry made a lunging, spinning backhanded catch, as Stan dove to the ground to avoid a collision. If Moore had missed the ball, DiMaggio may well have had an inside-the-park homer.

In the next inning, Gordon made a bid for a home run, but Musial got over to take the ball with his back against the grandstand wall. The very next batter, Keller, lifted a long fly to right. Slaughter ran to the low fence, boosted himself up with his bare hand, and made a leaping, glove-hand catch to snatch another potential home run away.

Spud Chandler pitched as well or better than White but took the loss. The only run he allowed came in the third inning, when the Cards did not get the ball out of the infield. Kurowski led off with a walk, and Marion sacrificed along the first-base line. But McCarthy and the Yankees coaches argued that the ball had been foul.

Lo and behold, the umpires reversed their decision and ordered Marion to bat again. This time Marty's bunt bounced high, and he beat the play for a single. White naturally sacrificed the runners ahead, and Brown's tricky grounder to second allowed Kurowski to score. The Yankees protest, seemingly on a trivial point, had backfired and cost them a precious run.

After Chandler went out for a pinch-hitter, the Cardinals added an insurance run thanks to a bad throw on another bunt. This one was fielded by the pitcher and thrown to second in time for the force. But the throw was too high. Ump Magerkurth, at second this game, made an initial call of "Out" but changed to "Safe" when he realized Rizzuto had been pulled off the bag. The Yanks stormed and strained against Magerkurth yet again, but the runner eventually scored. In the bottom of the ninth with two out and one on, Keller made another bid for a homer. It fell just short, and White had a 2–0 win.

The Cardinals were happy but not effusive in the clubhouse afterwards. White's statement to the press was brief but ungrammatically eloquent, "I feel gooder as hell. It was the greatest game I ever hope to pitch." In the Yankees' home clubhouse the mood was tight-lipped and grim.

Sunday's Game 4 brought out another World Series–record crowd of 69,902 paid. The majority of the fans paid $3.50 for general admission, and the Yankees were donating their share of the ticket proceeds for Games 4 and 5 to the United Service Organization (USO), a tidy $262,926.25. The $100,000 for radio rights also went to the USO. The games were also being carried to American servicemen across the globe with the help of the British Broadcasting Corporation (BBC).

Mort Cooper was back to make his second start for the visitors, while the Yankees called on Hank Borowy, a Fordham University product who had posted a neat 15–4 record in this his rookie season. New York took the lead in the first on a bloop double by Red

Rolfe and a line single by Cullenbine. But the Cards more than overcame that deficit with a six-run fourth inning. Musial led off with a bunt and outsprinted the ball to first, at least in the judgment of Magerkurth. Again the Yankees argued in vain. Walker Cooper followed with a hit up the middle, and Musial successfully challenged DiMaggio's arm and slid safely into third. Cooper never slowed down on the hit and made it to second on the play. This was definitely not the sort of baserunning the Yankees had encountered in the American League. By the time the inning had ended, three Redbirds had gone from first to third on singles, Musial had capped the rally with an RBI double, and St. Louis had six runs on the board.

Although Moore robbed DiMaggio of a potential triple in the Yankees fourth, the Bronx Bombers still had one counteroffensive to launch. They routed Cooper in the sixth inning with two singles, a walk, and a long three-run homer by Keller. And they nicked reliever Harry Gumbert for the tying run after a throwing error by Kurowski.

But the resilient Redbirds needed only three batters to break the 6–6 tie. Relief pitcher Atley Donald walked Slaughter to open the top half of the seventh then worked the count full against Musial. Ever aggressive, Slaughter broke for second on the next pitch. As catcher Bill Dickey was in the motion to throw the ball to second, the umpire called ball four. Dickey hitched his throw, but released the ball nevertheless, and it rainbowed into center field, allowing Slaughter to continue to third. Dickey was one of the greatest catchers ever, but now even he was rattled by St. Louis's relentless running game. Walker Cooper picked a good pitch and singled to center, and the Cards were back in the lead. Another run scored when Marty Marion fouled off four pitches before finally delivering a run-scoring flyball.

Southworth brought in Max Lanier to pitch. Max, nervous in Game 1, was cool and efficient in this outing. He pitched three scoreless innings, allowing just two hits, and he singled home an insurance run with two out in the ninth.

St. Louis had now won three in a row and was one win away from the title. Babe Ruth spoke to the Yankees in their clubhouse afterwards to keep their chins up. In 1926 the Cardinals had been facing elimination but they had come back to win, he told them. Now these Yankees would have to do the same thing.

The feeling was different in the visitors' clubhouse. Although none of the players dared to say it in public, Coach Mike Gonzalez was quoted as saying, "Tomorrow we will take the train to St. Louis, and we will be the only team on the train."

Going into Game 5, "We were a cocky bunch of Cardinals," Marty Marion later recalled, "but we wanted to do one thing. And that was to beat big Red Ruffing." The Cardinals may have knocked him out in the ninth inning earlier in the Series, but big Red had still notched his sixth consecutive World Series victory, establishing a mark that would last until 1968. To beat him would be like beating Bob Gibson a generation later.

It did not take long for the Yankees to give Ruffing a lead. Leading off the bottom of the first, Phil Rizzuto lined a home run down the left-field line. In the top of the second, Whitey Kurowski lined one into the same vicinity, but it hooked foul. Slaughter finally got the Birds into the scoring column in the fourth inning with a drive well up into the seats in right field, St. Louis's first home run of the Series. But New York regained the lead in their fourth round when Beazley threw wildly after fielding a bunt and DiMaggio delivered an RBI single. Another hit moved DiMag to third with one out but, after a conference on the mound with his manager, Beazley struck Gordon out and got Dickey on a routine grounder.

In the Yankees fifth, Marion, who had a spectacular series in the field, robbed Gerry Priddy of a hit. But then an infield dribbler and two botched double-play balls loaded the bases. Southworth again went to the hill to confer. Beazley came through again, retiring

Cullenbine on a pop fly and getting DiMaggio to rap a sharp grounder to third for the inning-ending force.

Buoyed by the escape, the Cardinals struck quickly to tie the count in the sixth. Moore and Slaughter each jumped on the first pitch and singled, putting runners on the corners. Musial popped out, but Walker Cooper delivered a long fly to drive Moore home.

The score remained 2–2 until the ninth, when Cooper led off with a single and Hopp sacrificed him to second. With first base open, McCarthy chose to have Ruffing pitch to Kurowski, and Whitey slammed a 1–1 pitch into the left-field seats, fair by several yards. It was his first home run since the key blow in Brooklyn three weeks before, and Kurowski was mobbed in the visitors dugout.

But the game was not over. The Yankees leadoff hitter in the bottom of the ninth was Joe Gordon, the AL MVP for 1942 who had had a miserable Series punctuated by seven strikeouts and no runs batted in. With one last chance at redemption, Gordon singled. Jimmy Brown bollixed Dickey's grounder, and the Yanks suddenly had the tying runs on with none out. Catcher Cooper called a mound conference to discuss strategy, telling shortstop Marion, "Watch it, Marty. We might try something." Priddy was the next batter, and as he squared to bunt Beazley buzzed one in very high and Priddy missed it. Gordon, trying for a good jump toward third, edged off too far, and Cooper instantly rifled a throw to Marion that picked him off. The air went out of the stadium with that, and the next two Yankees hit weakly to Brown for the final outs.

The Cardinals were World Champions! A loud clubhouse celebration followed, with particular attention paid to Southworth, Beazley, and Kurowski. Billy was nearly speechless trying to praise his boys. Beazley gushed, "Hot damn, I can't believe it's all true. But I guess it is. And won't Mom get a helluva kick out of this."

And Whitey would not let go of his home run bat, even when his teammates tore his pants off in glee. Mike Gonzalez had been right: Only one team took the train to St. Louis that night.

In the off-season, Rickey left the Cardinals to take over as president and general manager of the Dodgers before the end of October. Many stars went into the service over the winter, including Slaughter, Moore, and Beazley. But the well-stocked Cardinals farm system produced three more pennants in the next four years. Both New York and St. Louis won easy pennants in 1943, but it was the Yankees, hungry for revenge, who dominated the rematch in the World Series, turning the tables and winning in five games.

1942 Line Scores

Game 1, Wednesday, September 30, at Sportsman's Park, St. Louis

	1 2 3 4 5 6 7 8 9	R	H	E
New York	0 0 0 1 1 0 0 3 2	7	11	0
St. Louis	0 0 0 0 0 0 0 0 4	4	7	4

W—Ruffing L—M. Cooper
Time—2:35 Attendance—34,769

Summary: Joe DiMaggio scored two of the first three runs and drove in the other. St. Louis errors led to the final four New York tallies. Red Ruffing, meanwhile, took a no-hitter into the eighth inning and was one out away from a two-hit shutout when the Cardinals bats came alive. Four runs were scored and the bases were loaded before Spud Chandler finally retired the last batter.

Game 2, Thursday, October 1, at Sportsman's Park

	1 2 3 4 5 6 7 8 9	R	H	E
New York	0 0 0 0 0 0 0 3 0	3	10	2
St. Louis	2 0 0 0 0 0 1 1 x	4	6	0

W—Beazley L—Bonham
Time—1:57 Attendance—34,255

Summary: Walker Cooper's two-run double and Whitey Kurowski's RBI triple staked Beazley to a 3–0 lead. But DiMaggio's run-scoring hit followed by Charlie Keller's two-run homer tied the count in the top of the eighth. Enos Slaughter put the Cards ahead again in the bottom half by doubling, hustling to third on a missed relay throw, and scoring on a short single by Stan Musial. Slaughter then saved the lead by throwing out a pinch-runner trying for third base in the top of the ninth.

Game 3, Saturday, October 3, at Yankee Stadium, New York

	1 2 3 4 5 6 7 8 9	R	H	E
St. Louis	0 0 1 0 0 0 0 0 1	2	5	1
New York	0 0 0 0 0 0 0 0 0	0	6	1

W—White L—Chandler
Time—2:30 Attendance—69,123 (a new World Series record)

Summary: Left-hander Ernie White handed the Yankees their first shutout defeat in World Series play since the Cardinals' Jess Haines blanked them in 1926. Chandler pitched a strong game for New York as well, but a walk, two bunts, and an infield grounder in the third inning plated the only run White needed.

Game 4, Sunday, October 4, at Yankee Stadium

	1 2 3 4 5 6 7 8 9	R	H	E
St. Louis	0 0 0 6 0 0 2 0 1	9	12	1
New York	1 0 0 0 0 5 0 0 0	6	10	1

W—Lanier L—Donald

Time—2:28 Attendance—69,902 (breaking Series record of day before)

Summary: The Redbirds routed Yankees starter Hank Borowy in the fourth inning, scoring six runs on six hits and two walks. Musial opened that inning with a bunt single and capped it with an RBI double. But Keller's three-run homer routed Mort Cooper in the sixth, and an unearned run tied the count at 6–6. The Cards bounced back with two in the seventh, and Max Lanier made the lead stand up with three scoreless innings to close out the game.

Game 5, Monday, October 5, at Yankee Stadium

	1 2 3 4 5 6 7 8 9	R	H	E
St. Louis	0 0 0 1 0 1 0 0 2	4	9	4
New York	1 0 0 1 0 0 0 0 0	2	7	1

W—Beazley L—Ruffing

Time—1:58 Attendance—69,052

Summary: The Cardinals won their fourth game in a row to capture the Series, with Beazley pitching his second win. Whitey Kurowski's two-run homer gave the Birds the decisive lead. The first two Yankees hitters in the bottom of the ninth reached safely, but catcher Walker Cooper picked Joe Gordon off second base, and the next two batters were easy outs.

Total attendance: 277,101
Total gate receipts: $1,105,249
Cardinals player's share: $6,192.53

1944

Cardinals Defeat Browns 4 Games to 2

GAME 1:	CARDINALS	1	BROWNS	2
GAME 2:	CARDINALS	3	BROWNS	2
GAME 3:	CARDINALS	2	BROWNS	6
GAME 4:	CARDINALS	5	BROWNS	1
GAME 5:	CARDINALS	2	BROWNS	0
GAME 6:	CARDINALS	3	BROWNS	1

REGULAR-SEASON STARTING LINEUP		
Johnny Hopp	cf	.336
Ray Sanders	1b	.295, 102 RBIs
Stan Musial	rf	.347
Walker Cooper	c	.317
Whitey Kurowski	3b	20 HRs, All Star
Danny Litwhiler	lf	82 RBIs
Marty Marion	ss	NL MVP
Dutch Verban	2b	105 double plays

PITCHERS		
Mort Cooper	22-7	7 shutouts, 2.46 ERA
Ted Wilks	17-4	.810 winning percentage
Harry Brecheen	16-5	2.86 ERA
Max Lanier	17-12	141 Ks
Fred Schmidt	7-3	top reliever
Blix Donnelly	2-1	30-year-old rookie reliever

BENCH	
Ken O'Dea	c-ph
Augie Bergamo	of

How the Cardinals Got to the World Series:

The Cardinals easily won their third straight pennant under Manager Billy Southworth. After winning 91 of their first 121 games and building a 20-game lead the Redbirds went into a September slump and finished 14½ games ahead of second-place Pittsburgh. Their 105 victories marked the third straight year in which the Cardinals had won more than 100 games, a first for an NL team.

The Cardinals' Series Opponent:

For the only time in their fifty-two seasons in St. Louis, the Browns won the American League pennant. They did so under the gentlemanly Luke Sewell, who'd played for twenty years and appeared in the World Series with the Washington Senators in 1933. Sewell had guided the Browns since 1941. They won with an 89–65 record, same as the Cardinals had in their first pennant-winning season of 1926. It was at the time the lowest winning percentage for any AL pennant winner.

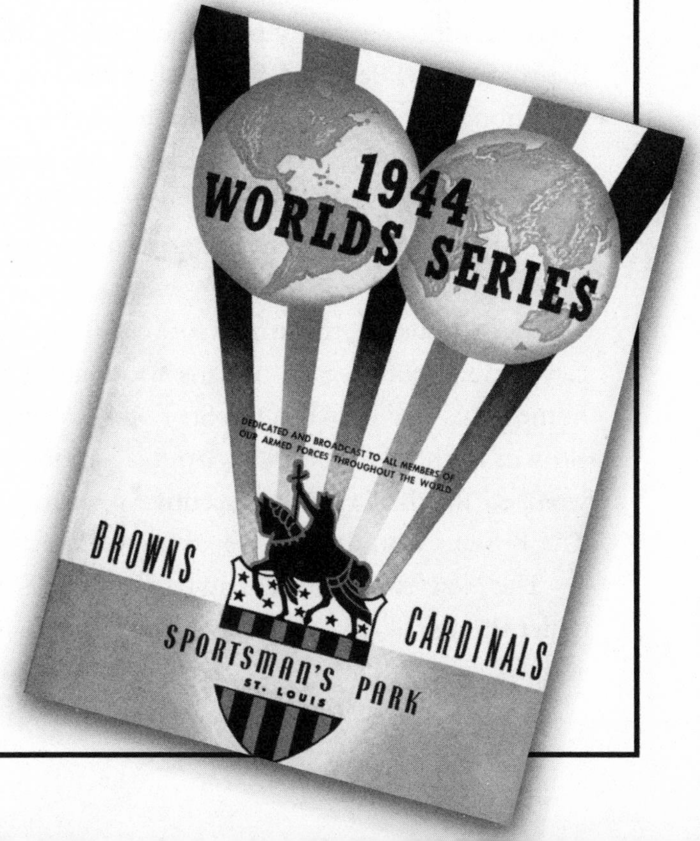

Meet Us in St. Louis

St. Louisans were in a happy mood the first week of October 1944.

Large headlines across the front pages in the city's three daily newspapers—the morning *Globe-Democrat* as well as the evening *Post-Dispatch* and *Star-Times*—proclaimed that the Allied Forces' planes, tanks, artillery, and infantry were blasting through Nazi defenses and into Germany near Aachen. St. Louis boys were among the soldiers, while those back home were manufacturing the ammunition they needed. Such places as the U.S. Cartridge Small Arms Plant, Curtiss-Wright Airplane Corporation, or Amertorp Torpedo Factory were just three of more than thirty factories in St. Louis that contracted with the government to provide war-related products.

Right beneath those newspaper stories of victorious American combat troops, St. Louisans also read of an impending war at home—this one between the St. Louis Cardinals and the St. Louis Browns in the World Series. Around Labor Day the Cardinals had wrapped up their third consecutive pennant, their eighth overall. The Browns won their first-ever flag on the last day of the season.

The New York Yankees had had several "Subway Series" against either the Brooklyn Dodgers or New York Giants; Chicago's Cubs and White Sox had once met in what might be called an "'El'

Train Series." Now it would be St. Louis's turn to host a "Streetcar Series." All games would be held at Sportsman's Park, which the teams shared.

The Cardinals and Browns both had highly respected managers—Billy Southworth of the Cardinals and Luke Sewell of the Browns. Both had performed in World Series as players, Southworth with the victorious 1926 Cardinals and Sewell with the Washington Senators, who lost to the New York Giants in 1933. During the regular season, they even shared an apartment in Lindell Towers, since when one team was at home the other was on the road. A generous apartment dweller in the same building vacated his unit during the Series so each manager and his family could have a separate place.

But in 1944 many major leaguers—including such stars as the Cardinals' Enos Slaughter, the Yankees' Joe DiMaggio, the Indians' Bob Feller, and the Red Sox's Ted Williams—were in a military rather than a baseball uniform. The St. Louis–based *Sporting News* posted rosters for each team that showed the age and draft status of each player, adding the caveat that fans might expect those under age twenty-seven to be called up for armed forces duty. Nine of the Cardinals were listed either 1-A or available for "limited service" while the Browns had ten in those categories. Researchers have determined that 174 National Leaguers and 168 American Leaguers who'd had major-league experience before or during World War II were in the armed forces in 1944. That included nineteen Cardinals and fifteen Browns.

Many major leaguers of 1944 had been judged unfit for military service but were physically able to play baseball. Among them were third baseman Whitey Kurowski, who had a bone infection known as osteomylitis, and outfielder Danny Litwhiler, with a bad knee. Shortstop Marty Marion, who had back problems, was listed as available for "limited service." Kurowski would lead the team in homers with twenty; Litwhiler would finish second with fifteen round-trippers; and Marion would be voted 1944's NL MVP, mostly for his defensive play that led to his nickname, "Mr. Shortstop."

"(Baseball) will go on with 4-F players, with over-age men, with youngsters of baseball precocity not yet registered for the draft," New York sportswriter Dan Daniel wrote in the *Sporting News* the week before the 1944 season began. "It will battle on not only in spite of reduced manpower, in spite of transportation difficulties, in spite of hotel troubles. It will fight on because there lies, inherent in this great game of ours, a definite spirit of continuity."

The administration of President Franklin D. Roosevelt repeated its support for the national pastime shortly before the season began as a way to uplift Americans working hard at home to support the troops overseas. One good thing for those fans to look forward to in 1944 was the increase in scheduled night games, since the Army's blackouts for security against bombing raids had been eased.

Despite their disappointing drubbing by the Yankees in the five-game 1943 World Series, the Cardinals were expected to repeat as NL kingpins for 1944. They didn't disappoint. They won 75 percent of their games through the end of August; from July 8 through August 29 they were 43–9, never losing two in a row. They ended 105–49 for the second straight season, this time 14½ games ahead of second-place Pittsburgh.

Only two starting position players from the 1943 Cardinals squad, second baseman Lou Klein and center fielder Harry Walker, went to war, and they were more than adequately replaced by Emil "Dutch" Verban and Johnny Hopp, respectively. Five pitchers—Howie Krist, Murry Dickson, Al Brazle, Howie Pollet, and Ernie White—from 1943's team, who'd collectively contributed forty wins, were called to military service; newcomers Ted Wilks, with seventeen wins, and Freddy Schmidt and Al Jurisich, each with seven victories, would make significant contributions in their places.

The Browns, meanwhile, weren't given much chance to go any higher in 1944 than the sixth place they finished the season before. The Yankees, despite losing five starting position players and twenty-game winner Spud Chandler to the war effort, were picked to win again.

The Browns lost few of their key players. They had a solid infield with George McQuinn at first; Don Gutteridge, a former Cardinal, at second; slugging shortstop Vern Stephens; and steady-fielding Mark Christman, who'd lead AL third basemen in putouts and fielding percentage. All had either started or put in significant playing time in 1943. The outfield was a mix of over-thirties flychasers such Gene Moore, Mike Kreevich, and Chet Laabs (when he wasn't doing war-related factory work) and youngsters Milt Byrnes and Al Zarilla. The starting right-handed trio of Nels Potter, Jack Kramer, and Bob Muncrief was back on the mound. They were joined for 1944 by Sig Jakucki and Tex Shirley, known as much for their bar-hopping hell-raising than for pitching; Jakucki hadn't pitched in the majors since 1936, and Shirley had been out of the game in 1943.

The Browns ignited local fan interest by winning their first nine games and setting the then-AL record for most consecutive wins to start a season. They spent much of the summer in first place but were in second, just behind Detroit, as the season's final weekend began. The Browns edged past the Tigers by sweeping a four-game series from the Yankees in Sportsman's Park that final weekend. Laabs hit a pair of two-run homers, and Jakucki pitched a complete-game 5–2 victory on the last day to give the Browns a final record of 89–65 and the pennant.

St. Louisans weren't as bitterly divided in their allegiance for the Cardinals or Browns as were fans of borough-centered New York teams or the north-south split between Chicago's Cubs and White Sox supporters. Nevertheless, a newspaper survey of the thirteen early bird St. Louisans waiting outside Sportsman's Park to buy tickets for the first game of the World Series found them all rooting for the Browns. Fans from around the country would send the Browns good luck charms. But as one local fan told the *Globe-Democrat*: "The chief thing that is wrong, they don't have anybody to razz. Sure, most of 'em want the Browns to win, but they like the Cardinals, too. Now if it was the Dodgers out there or the Giants . . ."

Players would note during the Series that the crowd seemed to favor the Browns; while the fans stood before both the top and bottom of the seventh inning, observing the then-custom for fans of the visitors and home team, one newspaperman said the first game had a "Browns tinge" to it. And while the Cardinals were the favorites, some observers noted that the Browns' pitching might be up for the challenge.

For Cardinals manager Southworth, the only choice for first-game hurler was Mort Cooper, his ace for the three pennant-winning seasons. Cooper had been MVP in 1942 but had lost the 1943 and 1944 All-Star Games, as well as the last game of the 1943 World Series, and had developed the reputation of not being able to beat the American League. Because of persistent arm pain he often chewed aspirin tablets during a game. His brother Walker was his catcher, as he had been during the two previous pennant-winning seasons.

The Browns' skipper, Sewell, was described by the *Sporting News* as someone whose "well-polished English" nevertheless couldn't hide the Alabama native's Southern accent. When not in a baseball uniform, he might have been taken for "a soil conservation instructor at Mississippi A&M or a business executive from Birmingham," the sports weekly stated. Sewell admitted that he made mistakes but added that if he'd been perfect as a manager "it would have been a pretty dull race." He let each of his players "stick to his strong points," and his players appreciated that. They also marveled at how he'd kept his hell-raisers, particularly Jakucki, in line.

Nevertheless, Sewell surprised observers by naming Denny Galehouse as his first-game starter instead of Nels Potter, who'd led the Browns with a 19–7 record and 2.83 ERA. Galehouse had been working in an armaments factory in his native Ohio during the week and pitching for the Browns on weekends until midseason. Then, after conferring with his draft board, he'd decided to chance selection before the end of the season and join the Browns full time. With a 9–10 mark, he was also the only pitcher up to that time to have a less than .500 regular-season record and be named to start the first game of a World Series.

Morning rain on Wednesday, October 4, gave way to afternoon sun and temperatures that climbed into the low eighties, about ten degrees warmer than usual, as the crowd settled in for the first pitch. They mixed a few boos among the cheers when the Cardinals came out for their warm-ups. But the capacity crowd of more than 33,000 gave "an enthusiastic roar" for the Browns when they stepped onto the field.

Amid those watching was a "generous sprinkling of Army and Navy uniforms." The Republican vice presidential candidate, Ohio Governor John Bricker, posed with Galehouse in a photo that made the front page of the Republican-leaning *Globe-Democrat* but not the Democratic-favoring *Post-Dispatch*. The presidential election between incumbent Democrat Franklin Delano Roosevelt and Republican Thomas Dewey was a month away. Dewey was proposing postwar tax cuts to create jobs and making vague accusations that FDR and his supporters were trying to turn the three-time incumbent into a monarch, charges that Roosevelt refuted.

Cooper, a big right-hander, was about as good as a pitcher could be that day. He gave the Browns only two hits, both in the fourth inning. Right-fielder Gene Moore singled to right with two out. First baseman George McQuinn, a left-handed hitter, "swinging from his hips," then sent a line drive "screeching to the right field (pavilion) roof" for a home run.

Galehouse gave the Cardinals five hits in the first three innings but stranded all the baserunners. With the bases loaded and one out in the third, he struck out Whitey Kurowski and induced Danny Litwhiler to ground out. Later, Galehouse would admit that he shook off his catcher, Bud Hayworth, only once. That was while facing Kurowski with the sacks jammed. With two strikes, Hayworth had called for a fastball, but Galehouse said he figured Kurowski would be looking for it so he threw—and got him with—a slider.

Once Galehouse had the lead he didn't allow another hit until the eighth and again kept the Cardinals off the scoreboard. The Redbirds pushed over a run in the ninth when Marion led off with a double, moved to second on a ground out, then scored on a pinch-hit run-scoring flyball by Ken O'Dea. Allowed to finish a game that a starter today would be yanked for, probably even before the ninth began, Galehouse threw 121 pitches in his 2–1 win.

Don Gutteridge, the Browns' third baseman and a Cardinal in the late 1930s, said later, "Cooper threw two fastballs (to Moore and McQuinn) but they weren't fast enough." Cooper countered to newsmen that the only good hit was McQuinn's and that Moore's single had "found a hole." He and McQuinn disagreed where the home run pitch had been, Cooper saying it was letter high, McQuinn calling it belt high.

Cardinals coach Mike Gonzalez, a Cuban, was quoted in the literal style of newspapers then: "They get 'em two heets, boom-boom, now bowl game over."

New York Telephone Company announced that 106,800 callers had asked for the score of the first game. The year before, 83,000 had called in for the score of the opener between the Yankees and Cardinals. Also, that very day, October 4, 1944, in Tampa, Florida, future Cardinals manager Tony La Russa was born.

The turning point of the Series for the Browns occurred in the second game, perhaps the biggest "what if" in the history of long-suffering Browns fans. Sewell confidently started his ace, Nels Potter, a righty, against the Cardinals' Max Lanier, a southpaw. Lanier had compiled a 17–12 record with a stingy 2.65 ERA despite having lost his last seven decisions.

Both managers tinkered a bit with their lineups. To give left fielder Danny Litwhiler's bad knee a rest, especially after the overnight rain would have softened the field, Southworth started Augie Bergamo and had him lead off. Sewell moved his left-handed-hitting first baseman, McQuinn, to fifth from sixth in the order.

The temperature again reached into the eighties and the crowd increased by nearly 2,000 from the day before. Both teams went down in order in the first and each had a base runner in the second, the Browns on a walk to McQuinn and the Cardinals on a double by Walker Cooper. But the game was scoreless going into the home half of the third.

Dutch Verban, the Cardinals second baseman, led off with a single, and Lanier followed with a sacrifice bunt attempt that Potter pounced on. But the pitcher's hurried throw after he bobbled it went into right field, allowing Lanier to reach and Verban to race to third, from where he scored on Bergamo's ground out. Verban an inning later would give the Cardinals their second run with a run-scoring flyball with the bases loaded. That run was also unearned because of a botched potential double-play ground ball by the Browns third baseman that had loaded the bases with one out.

Meanwhile, Lanier appeared to be cruising, not allowing a hit until a harmless leadoff single by Gene Moore in the fifth. Lanier carried a 2–0 shutout into the seventh. After retiring the first two hitters easily, he gave up another single to Moore. This time the Browns right fielder came around to score as catcher Red Hayworth doubled, and Hayworth then scored the tying run when pinch-hitter Frank Mancuso singled him home.

Bob Muncrief then took the mound for the Browns and retired the Cardinals in order in the seventh. Lanier's mastery of the Browns, however, was ending. After Mike Kreevich smacked a double to lead off the top of the eighth, Southworth summoned Blix Donnelly from the bullpen.

Sylvester Urban Donnelly, a thirty-year-old rookie right-hander that season, said he didn't know why his father, a semi-pro baseball player, had nicknamed him "Blix" or what it meant. Southworth had almost called in another reliever in that situation, Bud Byerly; but shortstop Marty Marion had pleaded with his manager to call Donnelly instead, who'd only thrown about a half-dozen warm-ups. "Byerly's got a bad leg and they'll be bunting on him," Marion said, persuading his manager.

Donnelly was 5 feet, 10 inches tall and weighed about 165 pounds, but managers all through his minor-league career had told him he was too small. He'd pitched the final two perfect innings in relief the day before, fanning two. Now he came to the mound "ripping mad," as he told the *Sporting News.* "I wanted to show Billy Southworth I could pitch like that. Nobody ever believed. They'd take one look at me and say with a compassionate look, 'Too bad he's so small.' Too small—that's all I've heard all my baseball life."

What he'd hear this day were oo's and ah's. He struck out the first two men he faced, Laabs and cleanup hitter Vern Stephens. Donnelly intentionally walked McQuinn then fanned Christman to end the threat.

Muncrief and Donnelly then dueled into extra innings. The Browns hurler was helped by two double plays in his four full innings. Donnelly used his fastball to whiff seven batters in his four frames. But perhaps Blix's most important contribution was a pinpoint throw he made to cut down McQuinn at third base after he'd led off the eleventh inning with a double and tried to move up on Christman's attempted sacrifice bunt.

In the home half of that inning, Cardinals first baseman Ray Sanders led off with a single and was sacrificed to second by Kurowski. Muncrief intentionally walked Marion, then faced Ken O'Dea coming off the bench to pinch-hit for Verban. In the first game, O'Dea helped the Cardinals avoid a shutout by hitting a run-scoring flyball in the ninth; now he promptly singled to right field, giving them a win that tied the Series at a game each.

In the ebb and flow of things, the Cardinals seemed to have captured the momentum as the third game began. They were now the "visitors," batting first for the next three games. Taking advantage of the Browns' now shaky defense, Johnny Hopp got to second on an error by Stephens at short, then with two out he scored when cleanup hitter Walker Cooper smacked a single to left off starter Jack Kramer, who was 17–13 on the year and whose 2.49 ERA had been the best among the team's regular starters.

The temperature reached an uncomfortable 88 degrees, causing girls in the bleachers to take off their shoes and socks while young men in that section took off their shirts. Among the dignitaries attending were Senator Harry S Truman of Missouri, the Democratic vice presidential running mate of Roosevelt. Perhaps to outdo his Republican rival Bricker, who'd attended the first game, Truman sat through both the second and third games.

One dignitary who wasn't there but would ordinarily have been was Baseball Commissioner Kenesaw Mountain Landis. The former federal judge had ruled baseball with an iron fist since the owners created the job in 1920. He was hospitalized in Chicago because of complications following a cold and was listening to the game on the Mutual Radio Network.

Wilks was a twenty-eight-year-old rookie, someone with a good fastball who'd been primarily a starter for the Cardinals that year and had compiled a 17–4 record in 1944. After retiring the Browns in order in the first without their hitting the ball out of the infield, he walked the bases loaded with two outs in the second before striking out mound foe Kramer to end the inning. He seemed to have gotten back on track when he caught Gutteridge looking at strike three to begin the home third and got Kreevich to fly out. But then the floodgates opened.

In quick succession Moore, Stephens, McQuinn, Zarilla, and Christman hit consecutive singles off Wilks, giving the Browns a

3–1 lead and drawing the hook from Southworth. "That third-inning explosion took place too quickly for me to do anything about it," the Cardinals manager offered later. Fred Schmidt replaced Wilks on the mound. After an intentional walk, he threw a wild pitch that allowed the fourth run to score.

In the meantime, Kramer found his rhythm and retired ten straight Cardinals until the Redbirds pushed across a run in the seventh. But the Browns came right back to score two, one on a passed ball and another on a double by McQuinn off Al Jurisich, the third of four Cardinals pitchers. The Browns won 6–2; Kramer pitched the equivalent of a shutout since both runs were unearned. In going the distance, he gave up seven hits, walked two, and struck out ten, including two in the ninth. If the Browns had won that close second game, they would have had an almost insurmountable three-game lead.

The real losers for the day, though, were some scalpers who, because of lower attendance, had had to sell their $6.25 tickets for as low as $2.

Meet Me in St. Louis, a film starring Judy Garland about a St. Louis family preparing for the 1904 World's Fair here, had premiered in 1944. The World Series seemed to be a meeting place for the media, which were going beyond the traditional "press" designation since more than newspapers were covering the games. Reporters from twenty-seven states and three from Canada, were at Sportsman's Park. Among them were Joe Page of the *Montreal Star*. He'd covered the first "world's championship series" in 1884 between the Providence Grays of the National League and the New York Metropolitans of the American Association, a major league of the 1880s. There were also "seven movie outfits" and representatives of "three G.I. papers." Among them was Sergeant Bob Broeg, later sports editor of the *Post-Dispatch*. His professional rival and friend, Bob Burnes, was already sports editor of the *Globe-Democrat*, turning out front-page stories about the Streetcar Series.

Game 4 was the turning point for the Cardinals. Down a game with a dead offense, they had to do something. They didn't want to fall behind three games to one since only one team had ever come back from a deficit like that, the 1925 Pittsburgh Pirates. Southworth went with Harry "The Cat" Brecheen.

"The players started calling me 'The Cat' because I seemed to be pretty good with the glove," he later told an interviewer. "When the exhibition games started, Roy Stockton of the *St. Louis Post-Dispatch* started to write about 'The Cat did this' and 'The Cat did that.' It just kind of stuck on me after that and people knew me."

Sewell picked Jakucki, who'd won the pennant-deciding game the previous Sunday, to start Game 4 for the Browns. Big Sig retired the first batter then gave up a single to Johnny Hopp. In stepped fellow Polish-American Stan Musial.

One of the great mysteries is why Musial, already an MVP and a batting champ by 1944 and destined for a Hall of Fame plaque in Cooperstown, could tattoo the outfield walls of Sportsman's Park and opponents fields during regular-season and All-Star games yet hit only .256 in four World Series. Hitting .250 for the first three games, Musial measured the first pitch from Jakucki and drove it to the roof of the right-field pavilion, a two-run homer that would turn out to be all the Cardinals would need this day.

However, the Cardinals had won the pennant with defense as well as offense, and they would show their glovework right away in the home half of the first. After Gutteridge struck out to lead off the inning, Kreevich singled to left. Gene Moore then blasted one from Brecheen to deep right center. Hopp raced back toward the concrete wall and made a sprinting, backhand catch, then held out his hands to absorb the impact with the wall. Brecheen induced Stephens to ground out.

The Cardinals would add a pair of runs in the third and a single run in the sixth. Brecheen would never have a 1–2–3 inning while giving up nine hits and four walks, but he would strand all but one baserunner. The Browns scored their only run in the eighth when Chet Laabs grounded into a double play, bringing Moore home from third.

One reason offered for the lack of offense for both teams in the Series was the white shirts of the fans packed into the center-field bleachers, ordinarily unoccupied except in sellouts. In this game, Laabs called time in the second and complained of something reflecting the sun into his eyes. The umps determined that the cause was buttons on the caps of two uniformed soldiers. The fighting men happily agreed to watch the rest of the game bareheaded.

The temperature had cooled by some fifteen degrees from the day before. The Cardinals were heating up, though.

Game 5 was a rematch of the opener: Mort Cooper vs. Denny Galehouse. It would live up to its billing as the pair of pitchers would set a record for strikeouts. Cooper fanned a dozen Browns, registering one in every inning except the fifth, while Galehouse struck out ten, notching one in all but the second, sixth, and seventh innings, as both starters went the distance.

The Browns starter gave up a leadoff double to Litwhiler and walked Musial but between them struck out Hopp then fanned Cooper and Sanders to strand two in the first. The Browns also put two on in the first via a hit and a walk but stranded both.

Both teams would put ample numbers of baserunners in scoring position, but the Browns batters would be zero for eight and the Cardinals none for seven in those situations. The only scoring came on a ball that Ray Sanders hit over the pavilion in the sixth and another that Litwhiler popped into the pavilion just to the left of where the screen ended at the 354-foot mark in the eighth. Both homers were solo shots. For Sanders, the team's regular-season RBI leader with 102, it would be his only run driven in for the Series. Litwhiler, moved by Southworth to the leadoff spot from his customary sixth place in the order "to take the pressure off him," responded with his second straight two-for-four day at the plate.

Both Galehouse and Cooper finished with a flourish: The Browns pitcher struck out the first two he faced in the ninth as part of a 1–2–3 inning; Cooper struck out three straight pinch-hitters he faced in the home half of the ninth—Milt Byrnes, Chet Laabs, and Mike Chartak. For the first time in the Series the Cardinals had the lead and needed but one more win.

Even home plate ump Ziggy Sears had good words for both hurlers afterwards, saying, "That was a masterful performance by both men."

Coffee was the beverage of choice for spectators at Game 6. The temperature, which had dropped to the mid-sixties the day before, now fell into the mid-fifties, making it seem like a day "better for football," opined the *Globe-Democrat.*

The Brownie bats, which had appeared to go into cold storage in scoring situations over the past few games, thawed temporarily in the second inning. Laabs tripled to deep center with one out, and McQuinn chased him home by spanking the next pitch into center. From there they managed only one more hit, a wasted double by Kreevich in the third.

Potter, however, kept the Cardinals at bay in the early going. After retiring the side in order in the first, he picked Kurowski off at first base to end the second inning after Kurowski had singled with two out. After Potter gave up consecutive one-out singles to Verban and Lanier in the third, the veteran screwballer then struck out Litwhiler and Hopp to end the threat.

Sloppy Browns defense, which had made eight errors in the first five games, figured in the Cardinals' rally in the fourth that gave them the lead they never relinquished. Cooper walked with one out then went to third on Sanders' single. Kurowski hit what could have been an inning-ending double-play grounder to Stephens at short, but the umpire ruled that Gutteridge, in taking the throw at second and relaying it to first, missed the bag, though Stephens would be given the error. Cooper scored and Sanders and Kurowski were on safely. The "daily Brown error . . . seemed to disturb Potter," the *Sporting News* observed.

Potter retired Marion on a foul fly to left, but Verban drove home what turned out to be the deciding run with a single to left. The Cardinals second baseman was called "the ugly duckling at the bottom of the batting order," whom the Cardinals had pinch-hit for late in each of the first three games. But Southworth let him play the final three in their entirety, and he responded by getting seven hits in seventeen times at-bat to lead all Series hitters with a .412 batting average.

Lanier then ended Potter's day by driving a ground single into left on which Kurowski scored the third run of the inning—all unearned but counting just the same.

The Browns would have one more chance. With one gone in the sixth, Lanier walked Laabs and McQuinn. He then uncorked a wild pitch with Christman at bat, putting the tying runs in scoring position and causing Southworth to bring Ted Wilks out of the bullpen. Wilks, driven out of the third game by a flurry of Browns singles, got Christman to tap to Kurowski at third, and his throw nailed Laabs at the plate. Hayworth then ended the inning by flying out to Hopp in center.

From there, Wilks gave a preview of why he would soon be nicknamed "The Big Cork" for his ability to come out of the bullpen and contain the opposition—this was long before the era of the "closer," and the save as a statistic. He retired the side in order in the seventh, eighth, and ninth, striking out the last two batters to put an exclamation point on his perfect eleven-batter performance. The Cardinals were champions of the world for the fifth time.

It had taken the Cardinals twenty-four years to get to their first World Series. Over the nineteen seasons that followed they became the most successful NL World Series team, a title they have yet to relinquish.

Both the Cardinals and Browns looked forward to even better days, but only the Cardinals would see them. Losing Musial to military service, the Cardinals dropped to second behind the Cubs in 1945; but when America's servicemen returned in 1946 the team would win another pennant and World Series. The 1945 Browns would feature a one-armed outfielder, Pete Gray, who helped attendance but became an object of ridicule and dissension among his own teammates, who felt using him had kept better players out of the lineup and doomed the team's pennant chances. They finished third, and nine years later they left St. Louis for Baltimore, ridding themselves of the Browns name and futile ways by assuming the Orioles moniker.

Commissioner Landis died in St. Luke's Hospital in Chicago on November 25, 1944. His successor, Senator A. B. "Happy" Chandler of Kentucky would in 1947 oversee the breaking of the barrier that had prevented blacks from playing in the major leagues.

1944 Line Scores

Game 1, Wednesday, October 4, at Sportsman's Park, St. Louis

	1	2	3	4	5	6	7	8	9	R	H	E
Browns	0	0	0	2	0	0	0	0	0	2	2	0
Cardinals	0	0	0	0	0	0	0	0	1	1	7	0

W—Galehouse L—Cooper
Time—2:05 Attendance—33,242

Summary: Surprise choice Denny Galehouse held off Cardinals while Browns made best of only hits, single by Gene Moore and homer by George McQuinn.

Game 2, Thursday, October 5, at Sportsman's Park

	1	2	3	4	5	6	7	8	9	10	11	R	H	E
Browns	0	0	0	0	0	0	2	0	0	0	0	2	7	4
Cardinals	0	0	1	1	0	0	0	0	0	0	1	3	7	0

W—Donnelly L—Muncrief
Time—2:32 Attendance—35,076

Summary: Blix Donnelly's perfect peg on sacrifice attempt in the eleventh nipped Browns rally while Ken O'Dea's pinch single won game in bottom of inning to knot Series.

Game 3, Friday, October 6, at Sportsman's Park

	1	2	3	4	5	6	7	8	9	R	H	E
Cardinals	1	0	0	0	0	0	1	0	0	2	7	0
Browns	0	0	4	0	0	0	2	0	x	6	8	2

W—Kramer L—Wilks
Time—2:19 Attendance—34,737

Summary: Browns routed Ted Wilks early while Jack Kramer throttled Cardinals bats to give AL champs the Series lead.

Game 4, Saturday, October 7, at Sportsman's Park

	1	2	3	4	5	6	7	8	9	R	H	E
Cardinals	2	0	2	0	0	1	0	0	0	5	12	0
Browns	0	0	0	0	0	0	0	1	0	1	9	1

W—Brecheen L—Jakucki
Time—2:22 Attendance—35,455

Summary: Stan Musial homer gave Cardinals margin of victory in first while Harry Brecheen continuously frustrated Browns' rallies.

Game 5, Sunday, October 8, at Sportsman's Park

	1	2	3	4	5	6	7	8	9	R	H	E
Cardinals	0	0	0	0	0	1	0	1	0	2	6	1
Browns	0	0	0	0	0	0	0	0	0	0	7	1

W—Cooper L—Galehouse
Time—2:04 Attendance—36,568

Summary: Rematch of Game 1 pitching pairing resulted in combined strikeout record of 22 from both starters; solo circuit clouts by Ray Sanders, Danny Litwhiler put Cardinals in driver's seat.

Game 6, Monday, October 9, at Sportsman's Park

	1	2	3	4	5	6	7	8	9	R	H	E
Browns	0	1	0	0	0	0	0	0	0	1	3	2
Cardinals	0	0	0	3	0	0	0	0	x	3	10	0

W—Lanier L—Potter
Time—2:06 Attendance—31,630

Summary: Cardinals claimed world title by wiping out early Browns lead and keeping their bats in cold storage.

Total attendance: 206,708
Total gate receipts: $906,122
Cardinals player's share: $4,626.01

1946

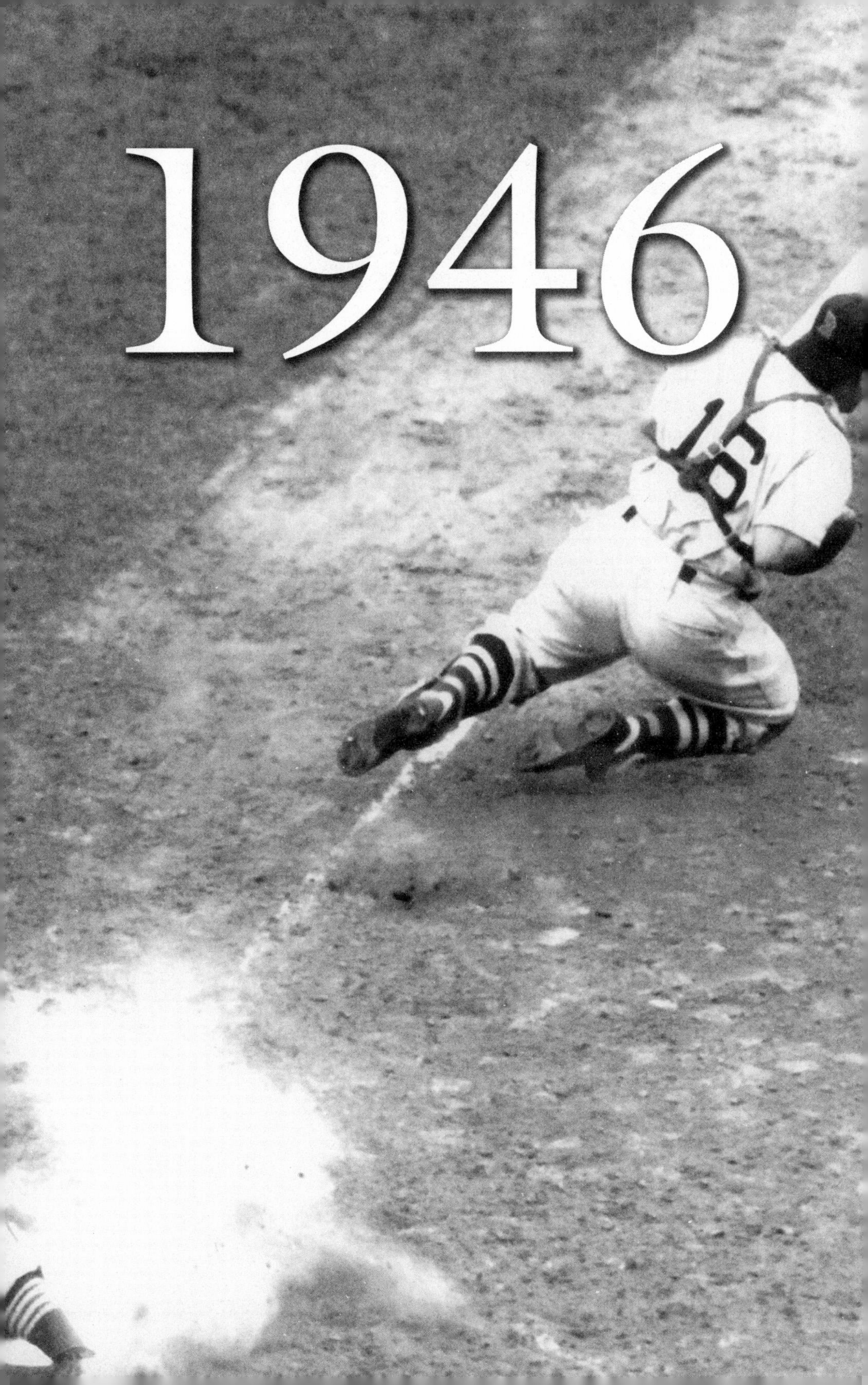

Cardinals Defeat Red Sox 4 Games to 3

GAME 1:	**CARDINALS**	**2**	**RED SOX**	**3**
GAME 2:	**CARDINALS**	**3**	**RED SOX**	**0**
GAME 3:	**CARDINALS**	**0**	**RED SOX**	**4**
GAME 4:	**CARDINALS**	**12**	**RED SOX**	**3**
GAME 5:	**CARDINALS**	**3**	**RED SOX**	**6**
GAME 6:	**CARDINALS**	**4**	**RED SOX**	**1**
GAME 7:	**CARDINALS**	**4**	**RED SOX**	**3**

REGULAR-SEASON STARTING LINEUP		
Red Schoendienst	2b	took over 2b in May
Terry Moore	cf	injury-plagued season
Stan Musial	1b	.365 average, NL MVP
Enos Slaughter	rf	NL-leading 130 RBIs
Whitey Kurowski	3b	.301, 89 RBIs
Harry Walker	lf	12 SBs, tied for club lead
Joe Garagiola	c	rookie at age 20
Marty Marion	ss	146 games, despite bad back

PITCHERS		
Howie Pollet	21-10	Led NL in wins and ERA (2.10)
Harry Brecheen	15-15	5 shutouts, 2.49 ERA
Murry Dickson	15-6	.714 winning percentage
Al Brazle	11-10	3.29 ERA
Ted Wilks	8-0	40 games pitched, 4 starts

BENCH	
Del Rice	c
Dick Sisler	of
Buster Adams	of
Erv Dusak	of
Clyde Kluttz	c

How the Cardinals Got to the World Series:

The Cards battled the Brooklyn Dodgers all season in a very tight pennant race. The contenders finished in a tie, necessitating the first-ever playoff to decide the champion. The Cardinals won the best-of-three matchup, two games to zero, to win the pennant.

The Cardinals' Series Opponent:

The Boston Red Sox started the season 21–3 and their early lead was never threatened. They finished 104–50 for their first pennant since 1918. The Sox had a solid four-man pitching rotation but featured a powerful batting attack centered around three 100-RBI men: Ted Williams (the AL MVP), Rudy York, and Bobby Doerr.

Slicing It Thin

With the end of World War II, the Cardinals seemed to be overloaded with major-league talent. At second base, for example, they had incumbents from three pennant-wining teams rejoining the squad: Jimmy Brown (1942), Lou Klein (1943), and Emil Verban (1944). And outfielders Stan Musial, Enos Slaughter, Terry Moore, Harry Walker, and Danny Litwhiler, among others, would be vying for playing time. This excess allowed owner Sam Breadon to cash in, and over the winter he sold nearly $300,000 worth of players to other National League clubs, most notably All-Star catcher Walker Cooper, who fetched $175,000 from the Giants.

Manager Billy Southworth had been allowed to take a three-year deal to manager the Boston Braves after the 1945 season ended, so the team needed a new manager. Breadon's choice was Eddie Dyer, an ex-pitcher who had managed Cardinals minor-league teams for fourteen seasons before being named farm director in 1943. A former baseball and football star at Rice, he had quit baseball in 1944 and was in the oil business in Houston when Sam convinced him to come back to manage in the big leagues.

St. Louis was the overwhelming favorite to win the NL pennant, picked by a whopping 114 out of 118 sportswriters in a pre-season Associated Press poll. But things began to go wrong for Dyer and the Redbirds almost from the start. The new skipper's shrill manner and excitable temper irritated some veterans and made some youngsters nervous. Third sacker Whitey Kurowski missed most of spring training as a holdout and was unable to play regularly for the first three weeks. Johnny Beazley, the Cards' Opening Day starter, was plagued by shoulder soreness. First baseman Ray Sanders was sold to the Braves (for $60,000), but his replacement Dick Sisler did not live up to expectations. Terry Moore's knee, Ken O'Dea's back, and Harry Brecheen's elbow all ached. On May 23 came the crushing news that three Redbirds, Klein and pitchers Freddie Martin and Max Lanier, had quit for higher-paying jobs in the outlaw Mexican League. Max Lanier, who was a perfect 6–0 as a starting pitcher with six complete games in six starts, would especially be missed.

Although St. Louis fell as far as seven and a half games behind Brooklyn in early July, the Cardinals lineup was starting to come together. Second-year man Albert "Red" Schoendienst had taken over as second baseman and leadoff hitter in early May. Late in the month a twenty-year-old St. Louis boy named Joe Garagiola got out of the army and took over much of the catching work. Musial was shifted from left field to first base in June and made the switch without losing any of his batting prowess. Hitting in the third spot in the order, Stan played every inning of every game in 1946, as did Enos Slaughter, who usually hit fourth.

As the players began to adjust to Dyer's style, he warmed up to them. After the end of the season Howie Pollet remarked, "Manager Dyer was never too busy or too worried to listen to players' troubles, and to offer worthwhile consolation and advice. And he was asked for plenty." Rookie Joe Garagiola put it simply, "Thanks for being a big brother to me."

Right after the All-Star Game, the Birds swept a four-game series from the Bums, and the race stayed tight right down to the wire. St. Louis edged into first place on August 22 and stayed there down the stretch. But Brooklyn stayed close and finally caught the leaders with two games left on the schedule. Both contenders won on Saturday, but both lost on the final Sunday, meaning the race had ended in a tie. A best-of-three playoff was necessary to determine the pennant winner. Breadon lost the coin flip, and the playoff was to open with one game in St. Louis then two games (if necessary) in Brooklyn.

The playoff opener at Sportsman's Park drew a disappointing 26,012, about 8,000 under capacity, but the game itself was a gem. Dyer called on twenty-game winner Howie Pollet to pitch, even though the Louisiana lefty had a painful torn muscle beneath his pitching shoulder. He was heavily taped around the chest by trainer Harrison "Doc" Weaver. Dodger manager Leo Durocher started young Ralph Branca, who had only three wins all season but who had beaten the Cardinals 5–0 in the rivals' final regular-season meeting. The Cards scored in the first inning when Joe Garagiola beat out a two-out, bases-loaded bouncer to shortstop. Dodger Howie Schultz homered to tie it in the top of the third, but St. Louis got two runs in the bottom to regain the lead. Whitey Kurowski out-hustled a potential double-play throw to allow the first run to count, then Garagiola and Harry Walker singled to plate Kurowski. Brookyn loaded the bases in the fifth, but Pollet got a double play to escape damage. Schultz drove in a second Dodgers run in the seventh, but Slaughter's throw from right nipped a runner at third to kill the rally. Garagiola drove in another run in the St. Louis seventh, and Pollet closed out a very gutty effort for a 4–2 win.

Game 2 was played in Brooklyn's Ebbets Field on Thursday, October 3. Needing to win only one of two, Dyer held back Harry Brecheen, who had been his most effective hurler down the stretch, and started Murry Dickson. The little right-hander yielded a run in the first inning but tripled home the go-ahead run himself in the Cards' two-run second. Slaughter's two-run triple was the key hit in a three-run fifth-inning rally that routed Dodgers started Joe Hatten. Called "Thomas Edison Jr." by his manager for his penchant for inventing new pitches as the situation changed, Dickson was cruising with an 8–1 lead going into the bottom of the ninth before being raked for three hits and a walk. Dyer rushed Brecheen in to relieve with two runs in, two men on, and only one out. The new hurler gave up a run-scoring hit and a walk, loading the bases and bringing the tying run to the plate. But the lefty struck out the next two men to seal the 8–4 verdict and give St. Louis its ninth NL pennant in twenty-one years.

Having been overwhelming favorites to win at the beginning of the season, the Cardinals went into the World Series as underdogs against the Boston Red Sox. Betting odds favored the Sox over the Cardinals by between 2–1 and 3–1. The Cardinals seemed to be underachievers. "I know a lot of folks thought we were loafing this year," Dyer said later. And veteran stars Marion and Moore were not 100 percent healthy, the shortstop battling a bad back, and the center fielder hobbled by torn cartilage in his knee. Boston, on the other hand, had no major injuries. Its powerhouse ballclub had made a shambles of the American League, leading by as much as seventeen games and coasting in to finish twelve games ahead. But the Red Sox lost twelve of their final twenty regular-season games and had to wait around for the NL playoff to end. To stay sharp, Red Sox management hired a group of American League All-Stars to play three midweek games against the champions. In first game, Senators left-hander Mickey Haefner hit Ted Williams in the right elbow with a pitch. The slugger's elbow ballooned and was still sore when the World Series began.

The World Series finally opened on Sunday, October 6, in St. Louis. When Williams went to bat in the second inning, the Cardinals shifted third baseman Kurowski over to the normal second-base slot, pulled the second baseman and center fielder into right field, and dared the Thumper to try to ram a hit through the crowded right side. Williams took the challenge and smacked one in the hole past first base. But second baseman Red Schoendient was stationed on the outfield grass and made an easy pickup and throw to first for an out.

The shift, a modification of a more radical shift used against Williams by the Indians, had been devised by Dyer with the advice of scouts Tony Kaufmann and Ken Penner. The pair had studied the Red Sox for several weeks and recommended pitching the slugger in on the hands against an overshifted defense. Williams had one hit and two walks in the opening game, though he did not figure in the scoring.

Rudy York and Pinky Higgins supplied most of the Red Sox offense in Game 1. Higgins got a lucky, check-swing RBI hit in the second inning and started the game-tying rally in the ninth with a bad-hop bouncer past shortstop. York provided the decisive blow with a two-out blast to the back of the bleachers in the tenth inning, and the Red Sox won 3–2.

The Cardinals bats did little against Red Sox right-hander Tex Hughson. Their first scoring chance came in the fourth inning, when Slaughter poled a two-out triple to right center. When the relay was mishandled, Enos came steaming around third toward home, but Coach Mike Gonzalez flagged him to a stop. The next hitter flied out, so Slaughter did not score. A scratch hit and a two-out RBI double by Musial in the sixth tied the game at 1–1. When a two-out fly got lost in the sun, the Cards took the lead in the eighth. Hughson was removed for a pinch-hitter as the Sox tied the game in the ninth. Earl Johnson, who pitched the last two innings, was credited with the win. Howie Pollet, still stiffly bandaged, pitched heroically, laboring through 140 pitches. But that one bad curveball that York hit for a homer beat him.

After the game Slaughter complained to his manager that Gonzalez's "stop sign" had cost the team a run. Dyer agreed and gave Enos a "green light" to take more aggressive chances on the bases. "I'll back you up," Eddie assured him.

Down a game, the Cardinals bounced right back by winning

Game 2 behind the pitching of Harry "the Cat" Brecheen. Listed as 5 feet 10 inches and 165 pounds, the left-hander looked even smaller because of a stooped-over delivery. He had a fastball and two speeds of curveball, but the screwball was his money pitch. He earned his nickname with his quick, agile fielding around the mound. He had been bothered by a sore elbow in the early season and had finished with a .500 percentage at 15–15 despite a stellar 2.49 ERA. At bat he had a paltry .133 mark, but he had won two separate 1–0 games by driving in the only run.

Since the Redbirds were thought to be vulnerable to southpaws, Boston manager Joe Cronin tapped lefty Mickey Harris for Game 2. Del Rice, the right-handed part of the St. Louis catching platoon, doubled in the third inning, and Brecheen promptly brought him home with a long single. The battery teamed up again in the fifth inning. Rice singled and Brecheen bunted. Third baseman Higgins threw wildly past second, and the runners galloped around to second and third. Terry Moore drove them in with a hot shot off second baseman Bobby Doerr's glove. The Red Sox had runners on base in each of the first five innings but could not get anyone to third base. In the last four innings, Brecheen allowed only one runner and finished with a 3–0, four-hit shutout. In batting practice, Williams had hit several balls onto the pavilion roof, but the Cat and the shift held Ted hitless in four at-bats in the game.

Game 3 took place back in Boston after a travel day. Murry Dickson pitched for the visitors, while Dave "Boo" Ferriss, a twenty-five-game winner, went for the home team. Dickson had a rough start. He complained that the photographers roaming the field interfered with his preparations, and he could not get sufficiently warmed up. With two on and two out in the bottom of the first inning and a full count, Boston's Rudy York lofted a high fly deep to left. The ball bounced off the top of the thirty-seven-foot fence and went into the net for a three-run homer. That was all Ferriss would need. He scattered six hits and one walk (never two in the same inning) and won easily, 4–0. Williams made headlines by bunting for his only hit. Cardinals star Stan Musial snapped an zero-for-eight stretch with a triple in the ninth inning but was left stranded.

St. Louis bounced back again to win Game 4 with ease, pounding out twenty hits and twelve runs. George Munger, who had been an army lieutenant until discharged in August, pitched the complete game for a 12–3 win, while six hurlers paraded across the mound for the losers. Slaughter opened the scoring with a 380-foot home run into the right-field seats in the second inning, and he later added a double and two singles. Kurowski and Garagiola also collected four hits, as did Boston leadoff man Wally Moses. That meant that four different players tied the existing World Series record for hits in a game. Slaughter scored four runs, tying another record. The Red Sox contributed four errors, while the Cardinals fielding was brilliant. Slaughter made galloping catches to his left and to his right and threw out a man at home from very deep right field. Moore in center made a sensational diving, rolling catch. "Mr. Shortstop" Marty Marion made the only St. Louis error, but he did contribute to victory with a neat squeeze bunt that scored an early run.

Boston came right back to win Game 5, taking the series lead for the third time. Joe Dobson, the Sox number four starter, got the assignment and pitched a strong game. Cards starter Pollet, on the other hand, lasted only one-third of an inning. Still suffering from the torn muscle on his left side, Howie was replaced by Alpha Brazle after just ten pitches. Pollet's final toss was lined through the shift by Williams for a run-scoring single, Ted's only RBI of the Series. An error by Boston shortstop Johnny Pesky and a hit by Harry Walker allowed St. Louis to tie the game in the top of the second. But the Red Sox regained the lead when Don Gutteridge singled Roy Partee home. Partee, a slow-footed catcher, was called safe after Terry Moore made a strong throw from center field, and Garagiola exploded when the call was made. Things got worse for St. Louis when Enos Slaughter was hit on the right elbow by a Dobson fastball in the fourth inning. The hard-bitten veteran refused to rub the spot ("I wouldn't give nobody the satisfaction of knowin' it hurt," he said) and even stole second base. But the elbow began to swell ominously, and he had to leave the game in the seventh inning. It was the first time all year that St. Louis did not have Country Slaughter in the lineup.

Leon Culberson, the Boston right fielder, lifted a home run into the screen above Fenway's famous left-field fence in the sixth inning, and shoddy fielding in the eighth helped boost Boston's lead to 6–1. Another Pesky error followed by another two-out hit by Walker made the final score 6–3. Walker had three RBIs in the game, while Dobson had allowed only four hits total and no earned runs.

While most of the Red Sox players hopped aboard an airplane to get to St. Louis for Game 6, the coaching staff and a few others took the train. Sam Breadon's men all traveled together by rail. Club physician Robert Hyland and trainer Doc Weaver spent much of the time treating Slaughter's injured elbow. Hyland warned him that he risked permanent injury if he tried to play in the next game. All year long the Cardinals had come back when the chips were down. Now Enos was determined to be in the lineup as they tried to do it again.

Slaughter indeed answered the bell for Game 6, played on Sunday, October 13, and was given a warm ovation by the Sportsman's Park faithful. Though in obvious pain, Enos contributed an RBI single and two walks. But the story of the game was Harry Brecheen. The Cat once again tamed the mighty Boston batting order, scattering seven hits but pitching out of trouble with the help of sparkling fielding by his teammates. Second baseman Red Schoendienst was in the middle of three picturesque double plays, and left fielder Erv Dusak threw out a runner at third base. Williams managed a walk and a single but was erased both times when York grounded into two twin killings.

The Cardinals batters chased lefty Mickey Harris again, this time in the third inning. Rice once again started things with a hit, and Schoendienst, Musial, Kurowski, and Slaughter added safeties to tally three runs. Only a spectacular shoestring catch in center field by Dom DiMaggio kept the count from going higher. Boston manager Joe Cronin rushed Tex Hughson in to relieve, and he held the Birds at bay through the seventh. But critics wondered why the nominal Red Sox ace had been brought into a losing game. York tripled and scored for the Sox in the seventh, but Marion's two-out run-scoring double in the eighth made the final score 4–1 in favor of St. Louis.

Monday was an off day, set aside to sell tickets, and on Tuesday, October 15, a standing-room-only crowd saw an epic Game 7. The Red Sox had Boo Ferriss, a shutout winner in the third game, well rested and ready to pitch. The Cardinals would counter with Murry Dickson, who had won the pennant clincher in Brooklyn. Boston got the first break and scored a run in the first inning when a bad-hop single scooted under Marion's glove to put runners at the corners. DiMaggio's long fly to right brought one man home, then Williams blasted one to straightaway center. The crowd held its breath, but Moore raced from his position in right center and flagged it down. Schoendienst opened the bottom of the first with a hit to left, and when Williams bobbled the ball, he tried for second. But Williams recovered quickly and pegged a perfect strike to second to retire the runner. One out later Musial doubled, but the Cardinals came away empty.

While Stan would finish the Series with a lackluster .222 batting average, five of his six hits went for extra bases, and he scored three runs and drove home four others. Ted, on the other hand, finished with five hits, all singles, and only two runs scored and one batted in.

The Cardinals tied the game in the second when Kurowski opened with a double into the gap and was moved around by an infield out and a long fly. In the Boston fourth Williams again tried to hit away from the shift, driving one over 400 feet to dead center field. This time left fielder Harry Walker snared it with an outstanding running catch. In the fifth Moore robbed Higgins of extra bases with another running catch near the wall.

In the home fifth, the Redbirds grabbed the lead. Walker's hot shot up the middle eluded Pesky. Marion sacrificed the runner to second. Dickson, he of the clutch hits in the Brooklyn playoff, delivered again with a looping double over third base, bringing Walker home. Schoendienst followed with a hot bouncer up the middle, and Dickson, running all the way, scored easily when DiMaggio fumbled the ball momentarily. When Moore followed with a line single to center, Cronin removed Ferriss and brought in Joe Dobson, who stanched the bleeding.

With a 3–1 lead, Dickson eased through the sixth and seventh innings. But Red Sox pinch-hitters opened the eighth with a single and a double, as Dyer scurried to the mound to make a pitching change. Although Dickson was reluctant to leave, his good friend and hunting buddy Harry Brecheen would try to save it for him, just like in the Brooklyn clincher. The Cat almost did it, striking out one man and getting the second to line to shallow right field. But Dom DiMaggio picked on a 3–1 screwball and blasted it off the fence in right center, driving home the tying runs. Pulling a muscle rounding first, DiMaggio only got a double on the blow and had to be removed for a pinch-runner. Brecheen now had to face Ted Williams. With nerves cracking all around the park, Dyer elected to challenge the slugger. The first pitch was a foul tip that broke catcher Garagiola's finger. A tense delay ensued as Rice suited up to take over the catching duties. On the next pitch, following Dyer's plans, Brecheen pitched one in on Williams's fists, and the anxious slugger lifted a high pop that Schoendienst caught in foul territory down the right-field line, ending the inning. The crowd had been loud rooting for victory all afternoon. Now the game was suddenly tied, 3–3, and a muted anxiety quieted the stands.

The new Red Sox pitcher was announced as Bob Klinger. National Leaguers knew him from his six years with the Pirates before the war. He had been effective in short relief for Boston in July and August. But his last outing had been a disaster on September 19. Pitching against the Browns right here in Sportsman's Park he had blown a lead and taken a loss without retiring a single batter. In almost four weeks since then he had not pitched for Cronin, not even in the tune-up games. St. Louis fans had new hope, especially after Slaughter opened the home half of the eighth with a solid single to center.

But Klinger retired the next two hitters quickly, and Slaughter remained at first base as Harry Walker came to the plate. A left-handed bat-control artist, Harry had already driven in five runs in the Series, leading the team. Now he called for a hit-and-run, and, with Slaughter breaking for second with the pitch, Walker lined one over shortstop and toward the gap. Hustling out of the batters box, Walker was determined to stretch the hit into a double. Center fielder Leon Culberson, just inserted to replace the injured DiMaggio, cut the ball off before it could bounce to the fence, and threw quickly to the relay man in short left field, Johnny Pesky. In taking the throw, Pesky checked Walker, but before he could throw to second, he realized there was a greater threat: Slaughter sprinting at full speed toward home plate. Remembering that missed opportunity to score in the first game, Country was not going to be stopped this time. Although the daring dash seemed likely to end in sure death, Pesky was caught off guard. The hurried throw to the plate was weak and well off line. Slaughter slid home safely while the ball bounced ten feet away.

The cheers were again stilled when the first two Red Sox got hits to open the ninth inning. Higgins tried to bunt the runners along but bounced one right to Kurowski near the third base bag. Whitey boldly ignored the easy force and tried for an around-the-horn double play. He got the force, but Schoendienst's relay to first was too late. So now the runners were at first and third with only one out. Brecheen got Partee to foul out, easing the anxiety slightly. Tom McBride was sent up as the Red Sox last hope. He had come through in exactly this situation in the ninth inning of Series opener, delivering a two-out single with men on first and third to tie that game. This time he slashed a grounder past the mound. Schoendienst got in front of it, but the hit rolled up his right arm. Red crimped the ball against his armpit, plucked it out, and flipped it toward short. Marion, covering the base, grabbed it an instant before Higgins slid to the bag. The out was made by a whisker, and the 1946 Cardinals, for all their trials and tribulations, were World Champions.

The roar from the fans was incredible . . . the breathtaking last out, the daring last run, winning in seven games after always trailing in the World Series, barely winning the pennant in a playoff. . . . After all the agony, the ecstasy was delicious. The bedlam in the clubhouse was delirious. When asked how it compared with his previous World Championships, owner Sam Breadon gushed, "I mean it. This was the best." And why not? The team's pre-tax profit was estimated at $1,150,000 thanks to record-setting attendance, booming concession sales at Sportsman's Park, and the sale of player contracts.

By the narrowest of margins, Breadon had postponed the demise of his championship club. *St. Louis Post-Dispatch* sports editor J. Roy Stockton observed, "No purveyor of salami ever cut his sausage any thinner than Sam sliced his baseball talent."

Breadon would sell the team after one more season and would die in May 1949. Relying on the likes of Musial, Slaughter, Marion, Pollet, and Brecheen, the Cardinals finished second in each of the next three seasons. But St. Louis would not be back in the World Series until 1964, eighteen long years later.

1946 Line Scores

Game 1, Sunday, October 6, at Sportsman's Park, St. Louis

	1	2	3	4	5	6	7	8	9	10	R	H	E
Boston	0	1	0	0	0	0	0	0	1	1	3	9	2
St. Louis	0	0	0	0	0	1	0	1	0	0	2	7	0

W—Johnson L—Pollet
Time—2:39 Attendance—36,218

Summary: The Cardinals took the lead in the eighth inning when Dom DiMaggio lost a fly ball in the sun, but the Red Sox tied it in the ninth after a bad-hop single. Rudy York's long homer with two out in the tenth won it for the visitors.

Game 2, Monday, October 7, at Sportsman's Park

	1	2	3	4	5	6	7	8	9	R	H	E
Boston	0	0	0	0	0	0	0	0	0	0	4	1
St. Louis	0	0	1	0	2	0	0	0	x	3	6	0

W—Brecheen L—Harris
Time—1:56 Attendance—35,815

Summary: The Red Sox were helpless against Harry Brecheen, and no Boston runner got as far as third base. Catcher Del Rice and pitcher Brecheen paced the Cardinals offense, as well, getting three of St. Louis's six hits and scoring all three runs.

Game 3, Wednesday, October 9, at Fenway Park, Boston

	1	2	3	4	5	6	7	8	9	R	H	E
St. Louis	0	0	0	0	0	0	0	0	0	0	6	1
Boston	3	0	0	0	0	0	0	1	x	4	8	0

W—Ferriss L—Dickson
Time—1:54 Attendance—34,500

Summary: York again got the decisive blow for Boston, a three-run home run with two out in the first inning, and he also scored the final run in the eighth. Boo Ferriss allowed only three Cardinals to get as far as second base, and two of them were then caught off base.

Game 4, Thursday, October 10, at Fenway Park

	1 2 3 4 5 6 7 8 9	R	H	E
St. Louis	0 3 3 0 1 0 1 0 4	12	20	1
Boston	0 0 0 1 0 0 0 2 0	3	9	4

W—Munger L—Hughson
Time—2:31 Attendance—35,645

Summary: The Cardinals tied the existing World Series team record with 20 hits, and three Redbirds, Enos Slaughter, Whitey Kurowski, and Joe Garagiola, tied the existing individual record with four safeties each. Slaughter opened the scoring with a solo home run and wound up with four runs scored, also tying a record. George Munger got the easy pitching win.

Game 5, Friday, October 11, at Fenway Park

	1 2 3 4 5 6 7 8 9	R	H	E
St. Louis	0 1 0 0 0 0 0 0 2	3	4	1
Boston	1 1 0 0 0 1 3 0 x	6	11	3

W—Dobson L—Brazle
Time—2:23 Attendance—35,982

Summary: Cardinals starter Howie Pollet had to leave the game after just 10 pitches and one run allowed. The Birds tied it with an unearned run, but Don Gutteridge's RBI single in the bottom of the second put the Sox ahead to stay. Joe Dobson limited St. Louis to four hits and three unearned runs. Slaughter had to leave the game after being hit by a pitch on the right elbow.

Game 6, Sunday, October 13, at Sportsman's Park

	1 2 3 4 5 6 7 8 9	R	H	E
Boston	0 0 0 0 0 0 1 0 0	1	7	0
St. Louis	0 0 3 0 0 0 0 1 x	4	8	0

W—Brecheen L—Harris
Time—1:56 Attendance—35,768

Summary: Facing elimination, the Cardinals were saved by stellar fielding and Brecheen's clutch pitching. The Sox got two hits in each of the first two innings but were turned away. The Cardinals knocked Mickey Harris out of the game with a five-hit, three-run attack in the third inning.

Game 7, Tuesday, October 15, at Sportsman's Park

	1	2	3	4	5	6	7	8	9	R	H	E
Boston	1	0	0	0	0	0	0	2	0	3	8	0
St. Louis	0	1	0	0	2	0	0	1	x	4	9	1

W—Brecheen L—Klinger
Time—2:17 Attendance—36,143

Summary: The Cardinals won the Series by taking a tension-packed seventh game. Starter Murry Dickson pitched brilliantly and hit a key double to put his team ahead in the fifth inning. He was relieved by Brecheen after two hits opened the top of the eighth. The Cat got the next two men out, but Dom DiMaggio came through with a two-run double to tie the score. Slaughter led off the last of the eighth with a hit, and after two quick outs, raced all the way around on a hit by Walker to medium-deep left center. Boston got runners on the corners in the ninth, but Red Schoendienst turned a tricky hopper into the game-ending force out.

Total attendance: 250,071
Total receipts: $1,052,900
Cardinals player's share: $3,742.33

1964

Cardinals Defeat Yankees 4 Games to 3

GAME 1:	**CARDINALS**	**9**	**YANKEES**	**5**
GAME 2:	**CARDINALS**	**3**	**YANKEES**	**8**
GAME 3:	**CARDINALS**	**1**	**YANKEES**	**2**
GAME 4:	**CARDINALS**	**4**	**YANKEES**	**3**
GAME 5:	**CARDINALS**	**5**	**YANKEES**	**2**
GAME 6:	**CARDINALS**	**3**	**YANKEES**	**8**
GAME 7:	**CARDINALS**	**7**	**YANKEES**	**5**

REGULAR-SEASON STARTING LINEUP		
Curt Flood	cf	NL-leading 211 hits
Lou Brock	lf	.348 after June trade
Dick Groat	ss	.292, 70 RBIs
Ken Boyer	3b	119 RBIs, NL MVP
Bill White	1b	.303
Mike Shannon	rf	9 HR in 88 games as rookie
Julian Javier	2b	injured for Series
Tim McCarver	c	.288

PITCHERS		
Ray Sadecki	20-11	3.68 ERA
Bob Gibson	19-12	287 innings, 245 Ks
Curt Simmons	18-9	3 shutouts, 3.43 ERA
Barney Schultz	1-3	11 saves
Roger Craig	7-9	4 saves
Ron Taylor	8-4	63 appearances 6 saves

BENCH	
Charlie James	of
Dal Maxvill	inf

How the Cardinals Got to the World Series:

The Cardinals won their first pennant in eighteen seasons, overcoming adversity caused by owner Gussie Busch's firing of popular general manager Bing Devine and threatening to can respected field manager Johnny Keane. The Redbirds drew on the experience of veterans energized by youngsters and a major trade that brought Lou Brock from the Cubs. The Cardinals began to jell in July and went 46–21 for the rest of season. The Cardinals especially surged in the final two weeks as the first-place Philadelphia Phillies blew a 6½-game lead. With a final record of 93–69, the Redbirds won the pennant by a single game over both the Phillies and Cincinnati Reds. St. Louis was in first place for only six days of the season—all in the last week—the shortest amount of time in the perch for any Cardinals pennant winner.

The Cardinals' Series Opponent:

The fabled New York Yankees won their fifth straight pennant—and fourteenth in the previous sixteen seasons. The Yankees, who finished at 99–63, had their most serious challenge over that stretch, nosing out the Chicago White Sox by a game and the Baltimore Orioles by two lengths. Yogi Berra, who'd grown up in the Italian "Hill" neighborhood of South St. Louis, managed the Bronx Bombers. Mickey Mantle (.303 BA, 35 HR, 111 RBIs), Roger Maris (26 HR), Joe Pepitone (28 HR, 100 RBIs), and St. Louisan Elston Howard (.313 BA, 84 RBIs) provided the offensive firepower; an aging Whitey Ford (17–6, 2.13 ERA, 8 shutouts) helped by youngsters Jim Bouton (18–13, 3.03 ERA, 4 shutouts) and rookie Mel Stottlemyre (9–3, 2.08 ERA after his August callup from the minors) steadied the starting staff. Pedro Ramos saved 8 games on a 1.25 ERA but was ineligible for World Series duty because he'd come over on waivers after September 1.

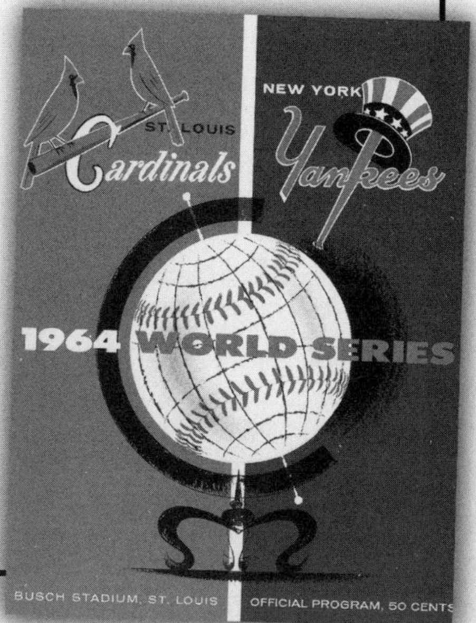

Gussie Grumbles, Redbirds Roost

Like the players on the Cardinals team that his brewery owned, Gussie Busch hated to lose. As the dog days of summer 1964 dragged on, it looked as if his Cardinals would come up short again in the pennant race. The Redbirds beat the Giants 6–4 on August 12, marking their thirteenth win in the previous eighteen games. But in those three weeks they'd remained in fifth place, still eight and a half games behind the first-place Philadelphia Phillies, who appeared to be cruising toward the flag.

Since Gussie had persuaded Anheuser-Busch's board of directors to buy the Cardinals in 1953, which made him president of the ballclub as well as the brewery, the Cardinals had finished no higher than second place, and that high only once, in 1957. This didn't sit well with August A. Busch Jr., who'd driven Anheuser-Busch to become the nation's largest brewer that year, a distinction it never relinquished while his family owned it. Busch predicted before 1957 that General Manager Frank Lane would be "out on his ass" if the Cardinals didn't win the pennant; shortly after they didn't, Trader Frank, as the always-ready-to-deal-a-player general manager had been nicknamed, moved on.

Seven years later, Busch was threatening to can Lane's successor, Bing Devine.

Devine, who had spent twenty-five years at various jobs in the

Cardinals organization, had built a respectable team for 1964 by both trading for talented players and having the sense not to deal away promising prospects the Cardinals' farm system had graduated. Through trades, Devine had brought to the Cardinals first baseman Bill White, second baseman Julian Javier, shortstop Dick Groat, center fielder Curt Flood, as well as veteran pitchers Curt Simmons and Roger Craig. He'd recalled veteran Barney Schultz, a knuckleball-throwing relief pitcher, from the minors in the beginning of August at the request of Manager Johnny Keane. Schultz had, under the rules then used, recorded eleven saves, which became a semi-official statistic in the 1960s after the *Sporting News* used it to determine a "fireman of the year" award for relief pitchers.

Meanwhile, the Cardinals' farm system produced such dependable players as third baseman and perennial All-Star Ken Boyer, who would be named NL Most Valuable Player in 1964; catcher Tim McCarver, a bulldog kind of player right from the start; right fielder Mike Shannon, who was from St. Louis and had been a quarterback for the University of Missouri Tigers; and pitcher Bob Gibson, who'd become the greatest pitcher in Cardinals history and enshrined in baseball's Hall of Fame. Gibson had benefited from Keane's confidence in putting him in the starting rotation shortly after Keane was named manager at mid-season in 1961.

Devine and Keane had worked well together, going back to their days as GM and manager at the Cardinals Rochester farm club in the early 1950s. When Devine told Keane right before the June 15 trading deadline that the Cardinals had the chance to get a young outfielder named Lou Brock from the Chicago Cubs, Keane replied, "What are we waiting for?"

The Cubs' "college of coaches," a musical chairs approach to managing the team, had thwarted Brock's potential. Under Keane's guidance, Brock was encouraged to be a base stealer rather than a home-run hitter. In his first two months with the Cardinals he raised his batting average from .251 to .300 and stole seventeen bases.

Despite the fact that the Cardinals players respected both Devine and Keane, Busch was no longer enthralled with either. The baseball-naïve Gussie had spent a couple million dollars refurbishing the old Sportsman's Park, which he called "a dump" when he first purchased it and renamed it Busch Stadium after fellow owners nixed his original plans to call it Budweiser Stadium. (His brewery also started brewing Busch Bavarian Beer two years later.) Gussie then waved big bucks—from $500,000 to a million—in the faces of fellow owners, hoping to buy some of their best players—Dodgers first baseman Gil Hodges, Cubs shortstop Ernie Banks, and Giants center fielder Willie Mays—only to be rebuffed on every attempt. After that he trusted his baseball men to do the job, while keeping a close eye on matters.

Busch could be irascible, but lovable, too. After becoming team president he joined his new team in spring training, wearing a uniform jersey and cap like theirs and posing for pictures with them. He oversaw the racial integration of the team with its signing of black players Tom Alston and Brooks Lawrence, then saw to an end of the practice of separate hotels for white and African-American Cardinals players during spring training. And he could laugh at himself, as he did when he displayed with a smile a book from a prankster friend titled, "'What I Know About Baseball,' by August A. Busch Jr." It contained four hundred blank pages. Gussie also talked about how he wanted to bring a pennant to "our fans."

But by mid-summer, Busch was frustrated and wanted a winner. He said publicly that the team could no longer depend on trades and that it should see more production from its farm system. Advising him on such matters as a special consultant was Branch Rickey, the team's general manager in the 1920s and 1930s who'd built the Cardinals' exemplary farm system—and who didn't like Devine.

On August 13, the Cardinals flew to Los Angeles to begin a western road trip. But Devine didn't go with them. Busch fired him. Several Cardinals players called Devine to express their regrets. Busch then not so discreetly sought the services of Leo Durocher, the shortstop on the Cardinals' Gashouse Gang champs of 1934 and pilot of two New York Giants pennant winners in the 1950s, to be the Cardinals manager for 1965.

After the season, some observers would call Devine's firing a turning point in the season. Others would say it was his trading for Lou Brock. But two crucial things happened in the last two weeks of the season that made such speculation possible. The Phillies, who had a 6½-game lead over both the Cardinals and Cincinnati Reds with twelve games to go, then lost ten straight. The Cardinals won nine of ten during that time. They gave the Phils their last three losses.

As the final weekend of the regular season began on Friday, October 2, the Cardinals were 92–67, a half-game ahead of Cincinnati and 2½ in front of Philadelphia. The Phils came out of their trance to nip the Reds that night while Al Jackson of the last-place New York Mets shut out the Cardinals, 1–0, at Busch Stadium. While the Reds and Phillies took the next day off in Cincinnati, the Mets pounded the Cardinals, 15–5, to keep alive the possibility of the first-ever three-way tie for first.

Philadelphia then humiliated Cincinnati before a big crowd on the final day of the season. The Cardinals spotted the Mets an early lead but came back to pound them 11–5, Barney Schultz relieving a tired but victorious Gibson in the ninth. In the top of the ninth, Cardinals radio broadcaster Harry Caray, with microphone, was sitting next to Busch in the owner's box near the Cardinals dugout. With two outs, KMOX listeners heard Busch in the background holler, "C'mon, c'mon, let's go, get 'im out, get 'im out!" And when catcher Tim McCarver squeezed the last out on a foul popup, Caray screamed what fans had yearned to hear for nearly two decades: "The Cardinals win the pennant, the Cardinals win the pennant, the Cardinals win the pennant!"

Busch shelved his plans to hire Durocher and instead immediately offered Keane a new contract for 1965. Keane, who'd attended Cardinals games as a kid through its Knothole Gang, said he didn't want to be distracted by contract matters during the World Series and would settle things with Busch when it was over.

The 1964 World Series matched two storied franchises: the mighty New York Yankees, who'd dominated October baseball for more than forty years, and the Cardinals, basking again in the glory they'd known from the mid-1920s through the end of World War II. *Globe-Democrat* sports editor Bob Burnes wrote before the Series began that the 1964 Cardinals were "perhaps not a great ballclub but certainly a most resilient one." Nevertheless, oddsmakers listed the Yankees as 17–10 favorites before the Series began.

The Yankees had been humiliated in a four-game World Series sweep by the Los Angeles Dodgers the year before and wanted to re-establish themselves as world beaters. Their manager, Yogi Berra, had grown up in the Italian "Hill" neighborhood of South St. Louis; the team's catcher, Elston Howard, the Yanks' first player of African-American heritage, had been reared in St. Louis's Compton Hill neighborhood, which his mother called a "soot-splattered neighborhood" near the old Scullin Steel plant. The team's third baseman, Clete Boyer, was a Missouri native and brother of the Cardinals third sacker, Ken Boyer. And they still had the M&M boys: Mickey Mantle and Roger Maris. Maris had hit twenty-six homers, a far cry from his record sixty-one of 1961, but had batted .281. Always dependable in right field, he'd made only one error in 141 games. In what would be his last great season, Mantle batted .303 with 35 HR and 111 RBIs. Toward the end of the season, to put less stress on Mantle's chronically bad right knee and legs, Berra began playing him in either left or right field rather than his customary center. For the Series, Mantle would patrol right while Maris was in center.

Some had questioned how Berra could be an effective manager of players who had been his teammates just the year before; some, like Mantle and Whitey Ford, had played alongside him for more than a decade. Berra had deliberately taken only a one-year contract for 1964, rather than the two-year deal he'd been offered. "I wanted to make sure I could do the job first," he told the *Sporting News* after having won the pennant. "I didn't want to stick anybody with a flop for two years." He gave complete credit to his players for winning the pennant. "I tried to do the best I could, but I never lost confidence in the players."

Cardinals great Stan Musial, who had retired the year before after a twenty-two-season career that would put him in the Hall of Fame, was quoted as saying that his successor in left field, Lou Brock, was the reason the Cardinals had won the pennant and that they wouldn't have won if he'd stayed around one more year. Musial, named by late President John F. Kennedy to head a national physical fitness program, was pictured with Yankees star Mickey Mantle on the Busch Stadium field; the photo caption stated that a smiling Musial had found a smiling Mantle "fit" for the Series.

The weather cooperated with a mild, sunny day and temperatures in the low seventies for the opener on Wednesday, October 7. Busch Stadium was filled to its 30,805 capacity that included standing-room-only tickets. The only blemish to the festivities was the conduct of a "shoving mass of boisterous gate crashers," as a newspaper called them, right before two-dollar bleacher tickets went on sale. Fans who'd waited in line patiently for up to twenty hours, some driving in from far away, were jostled by the last-minute intruders and denied the chance to buy tickets. Many of them criticized the police and the Andy Frain ushers on duty for not doing enough to prevent the fracas.

Whitey Ford, the Yankees ace for the previous decade, was Berra's choice for Game 1, while Keane countered with a southpaw of his own, Ray Sadecki, the Cardinals' twenty-game winner.

Sadecki had gotten in Keane's doghouse in June 1962 after

pitching and fielding poorly in a game the Cardinals came back to win; Keane called it "the poorest exhibition I've ever seen on a major league diamond." When Sadecki didn't come to the park the next night, he was suspended for a day and fined $250. But he'd gone on to patch things up and pitch effectively. Sadecki won two games during the Cardinals' torrid surge of the last two weeks of the 1964 season, including a 4–2 win over the struggling Phillies in the last week that put the Cardinals in a first-place tie with the Reds.

Neither starter was effective, though each lasted into the sixth inning. Both Sadecki and Ford got RBI hits off the other early. But as the Cardinals came to bat in the bottom of the sixth, they trailed 4–2. Ken Boyer led off with a single and moved to second on a passed ball. But Bill White fanned. Up stepped Mike Shannon, a product of local Christian Brothers College High School. Shannon had come up from the minors for good in July of the current season and become the Cardinals' regular right fielder. He'd hit nine homers in eighty-eight games; his first had been a big one—a solo shot on July 14 off Sandy Koufax at Busch Stadium that gave the Cardinals their first run in what became a come-from-behind win over the Dodgers. Called the "Moon Man" by teammates, Shannon put a Ford pitch nearly in orbit as it cracked the electronic lettering on the Budweiser sign high above the left-field scoreboard behind the left-field bleachers.

Tim McCarver's double brought Berra to the mound and lefty Al Downing out of the bullpen. Downing, who'd started thirty-five games, had made two regular-season relief appearances, gaining one save. He got pinch-hitter Charley James to pop out but then gave up an RBI single to pinch-hitter Carl Warwick. Curt Flood then chased home another run with a triple on a ball left fielder Tom Tresh had trouble tracking in the sun.

Barney Schultz, the Cardinals' bullpen stopper (the term "closer" hadn't yet been coined), took the mound and gave up a single to Mantle and walked Tom Tresh; but he stranded both by striking out first baseman Joe Pepitone. The Yankees would score once off Schultz in the eighth when Bobby Richardson's second hit of the game drove home pinch-runner Mike Hegan with two out.

The Cardinals, however, scored three in their half when Flood's two-out single drove in one run and Brock's double plated two more. The Yankees went down meekly against Schultz in the ninth and the Cardinals had the first game, 9–5.

The Yankees' main comments after the game were about how hard and fast the infield surface was at Busch Stadium. They also noted the "chewed up" grass in center field. Dick Groat, who'd played on the field all season, responded that he hadn't noticed the deficiencies the Yankees had.

Fans were "numbed by the cold" and a north wind as the Game 2 temperature was twenty degrees cooler than the day before. Rookie Yankees right-hander Mel Stottlemyre cooled the Cardinals' bats, limiting them to one run and three hits through the first seven innings. As Barney Schultz had rejuvenated the Cardinals' bullpen after his early August callup from the minors, Stottlemyre had done the same for the Yankees rotation since joining then August 12. The Yankees were in third place, 3½ games out on that date. Stottlemyre's 9–3 mark, which included five complete games, two shutouts, and a stingy 2.06 ERA, helped them outlast the White Sox and Orioles, both of whom he beat in his first two starts.

Bob Gibson started for the Cardinals and was almost as good as Stottlemyre for the first six innings. After the Cardinals scratched for a run in their third on two hits and a ground out by Flood, the Yankees loaded the bases in the fourth and Clete Boyer knotted the score with a run-scoring flyball.

The turning point, both managers would say later, came in the sixth with the score 1–1. Mantle drew a walk to lead off. Howard lined to Maxvill, filling in for an injured Javier at second base, who made a diving catch near the base. Gibson then came inside on Pepitone, who checked his swing on a 1–2 count. McCarver, the catcher, and the Cardinals thought the pitched nicked the bat. Pepitone stayed at the plate. But umpire Bill McKinley motioned him to first base and ruled that the ball had nicked Pepitone's left thigh. Keane led a displeased Cardinals infield in arguing the call, but it stuck. Tresh then singled into left and Mantle scored, giving the Yankees a lead they'd never give up. Later, Pepitone would say the ball did hit him. But he pointed to his other hip.

The Yanks added two runs in the seventh, but the Cardinals came back in their eighth. Carl Warwick, pinch-hitting for Maxvill as he had in the first game, reprised his performance by lashing another single. He went to third when Bob Skinner pinch-hit for Gibson and bounced a ground-rule double into the bleachers. Warwick scored on a one-out ground ball to short by Brock.

Down only by two runs, Keane turned to Schultz again. The Cardinals saw pesky Phil Linz ignite a ninth-inning rally when he could have been retired—twice.

Linz had filled in admirably late in the year at short for the injured Tony Kubek. However, Linz unfortunately is remembered mostly for a harmonica-playing incident that drew Berra's wrath. After the Yankees got swept in a four-game series by the White Sox in Chicago in mid-August, they headed for the airport on the team bus. Linz, sitting toward the back of the bus, produced a harmonica and began playing "Mary Had a Little Lamb." Berra, sitting near the front, told him to shove it. Linz didn't hear him clearly and asked what he'd said. "He said play it louder," a devilish Mantle told the shortstop, who kept playing. An angry Berra stormed back and swatted the harmonica when Linz tossed it to him then fined Linz. Player and manager later patched up their differences.

Now in the ninth inning of the second game that the Yankees needed to win, Linz popped a foul ball near the left-field line. Brock ran to it then dropped it on the bullpen mound. Linz next popped a foul near the third-base dugout that Boyer couldn't handle. Neither fielder, however, received an error. Third time was the charm for Linz, who then popped a home run into the left-field bleachers. During the regular season, he had hit five in 368 at-bats; this Series he hit two, both at Busch, in thirty-three plate appearances.

The Yankees would add three more runs off Schultz and southpaw reliever Gordon Richardson before Roger Craig would come out of the bullpen to end things. Stottlemyre would allow a run in the ninth but shut the door on the rally.

After a travel day, the Series resumed on Saturday, October 10, in Yankee Stadium. The low fifties temperature followed the teams. But it didn't affect the crowd, more than 67,000 of whom filled the venerable House That Ruth Built.

The Cardinals this day would depend on left-hander Curt Simmons. Simmons, now thirty-five, had missed his chance to pitch in the 1950 World Series for the Phillies team he had helped to win the pennant. National Guard duty had taken him before the World Series.

Now given his chance, he appeared to be making the best of it. He retired the side in the first, third, fifth, seventh, and eighth innings. In the second, Elston Howard singled with one out, moved to second when Pepitone walked with two out, and scored when Clete Boyer doubled. The only other chance the Yankees had to score against Simmons came in the sixth, when Richardson singled with one out and moved to third when Mantle doubled with two gone. Howard was intentionally walked, and Tresh popped out to White near the mound.

Jim Bouton, the Yankees starter, proved just as tough as Simmons, retiring the side in three of the first four innings and carrying a 1–0 lead into the fifth. Ten years younger than his mound opponent, Bouton admitted to having been a New York Giants fan while growing up and rooting for Simmons and Phillies teammate Robin Roberts every time they pitched against the Giants' hated rival, the Brooklyn Dodgers.

Bouton was five years away from penning *Ball Four*, the tell-all jock diary that would strain his friendship with Mantle and sever it with Elston Howard and others, while endearing him to readers who wanted to know what ballplayers did away from the park. Bouton had yet to injure his arm and develop the knuckleball that kept him around long enough to become an athlete-author. In 1964 he threw hard, directly overhand, and his right forearm follow-through often knocked off his cap. By someone's count, it came off 38 times in his 123 pitches this day. Berra said the club had gotten him to try different cap sizes in hopes one would stay on better. While observers wondered if it unfairly distracted batters, hitters such as the Cardinals' Dick Groat said it hadn't and that hitters had other things to be more concerned about.

In the fifth, two innings after the stadium lights had been turned on during the overcast day, McCarver led off with a single to right and continued to second when Mantle couldn't come up with the ball cleanly. Shannon followed by lining the ball to Mantle, who snared it. Maxvill then moved McCarver to third with a ground ball to the right side. Simmons then tied the game for himself by slashing the ball toward left field. Clete Boyer got his glove on it, but it got beyond him and was ruled a single.

It stayed 1–1 into the ninth. McCarver led off for the Cardinals by reaching safely when Linz at short couldn't handle his ground ball. Shannon then sacrificed McCarver to second. Warwick, batting for Maxvill for the third straight game, walked. Here Keane decided to go for the lead run and trust his bullpen, so he pinch-hit Skinner for Simmons. The former Pirate, who with Groat had battled the Yankees in the 1960 Series, skied one to deep center that Maris caught, allowing McCarver to tag and advance to third. But Flood skied one to Mantle in right, ending the Cardinals threat.

Different eyewitnesses give slightly different accounts of what happened in the Yankees half of the ninth. Keane again went to Schultz to hold things. Mantle, due to lead off, stood just outside the left-handed hitter's box watching the aging knuckleballer warm up. Berra would tell the press that he urged Mickey to hit a homer. Bouton decades later would tell ESPN that Mantle told his teammates he was going to hit a homer and win it.

One thing Mantle had been told by the Yankees scouts was that Schultz would throw his first pitch a little harder than usual trying to get over a strike. Mantle swung from the heels at that first pitch and lofted it into the right-field upper deck. Shannon, in right field, acted as if he had a chance to catch it.

Yankees fans jumped up and down in their seats. Schultz walked off the mound without looking back and long before Mantle crossed the plate to his teammates' glee. His sixteenth career World Series homer had just broken the tie he'd shared with Ruth. More importantly, it had given the Yankees a 2–1 lead in games.

"It was a knuckle ball. It wasn't a good one, I don't think," Mantle told reporters later. He added that he was glad the goat's horns wouldn't grow on him because of his earlier error.

"You throw just one pitch and it's gone," Schultz lamented.

Simmons absolved his reliever teammate of any blame. "He delivered countless times this year—and he certainly helped bring us the pennant," he said.

Keane meanwhile fretted about his team's lack of offense. That fretting continued in the early innings the next afternoon, Sunday, October 11. In the first inning, he also had to worry about the Cardinals pitching. After the Cardinals went down meekly in their first, the Yankees went to work on Cardinals starter Ray Sadecki. Linz led off with a double down the right-field line. A botched hit-and-run play then caused Linz to be hung up between second and third, but Ken Boyer's low throw back to second base allowed Linz to go on to third. Richardson then banged a double down the left-field line.

The Yankees second baseman then moved to third when Maris dropped a single in front of Shannon in right field. Shannon said later that he would have caught such a ball in St. Louis because he would have been playing more shallow; in Yankee Stadium, he was playing Maris deep to cut down extra-base hits into its right-center-field gap.

Mantle then sent Richardson home and Maris to third with a popfly single near the right-field line, but the Mick was gunned out at second on a good throw by Shannon. At that point, Keane put out the hook for Sadecki and summoned Roger Craig from the bullpen. The Cardinals skipper later acknowledged that Sadecki had given up "only one solid hit," but added, "I couldn't afford to take any chances."

Craig had gone through a late-season slump and was greeted by a run-scoring single by Howard, making it 3–0 Yankees with only one out. But Craig then fanned Tresh and induced Pepitone to fly out to right field.

Craig went on to pitch four scoreless innings, though he did walk three, two of them in the third. He got out of that inning in a most curious way. He walked Mantle and Howard with two out. While Tresh was batting, Cardinals shortstop Dick Groat struck up a conversation with Mantle, laughing at how Shannon the day before had acted as if he had a chance to catch Mickey's game-winning homer even though it had landed in the upper deck. Mantle laughed, too, and relaxed enough so that Craig wheeled and threw perfectly to Groat for a pickoff play that ended the inning. In later years, Mantle would remind Groat of that play, not in a joking way.

By the top of the sixth, Yankees and Cardinals fans must have had contrary emotions. A three-games-to-one lead, which both must have contemplated, was considered almost insurmountable. Only twice had a team rallied from such a deficit.

The Cardinals, however, were determined not to let that happen. Warwick, appearing as a pinch-hitter for the fourth straight game, led off batting for Craig and singled, thus tying a World Series record for pinch-hits in a single Series. Flood then moved him to second with an opposite-field single. Brock flied out. Groat hit what looked like an inning-ending double play to Richardson. But the usually sure-handed infielder, who'd led AL second basemen in putouts, couldn't get the ball out of his glove cleanly. When Linz couldn't handle his bouncing toss, Richardson was charged with an error. The bases were loaded for cleanup man Ken Boyer, one for thirteen with one RBI thus far.

Boyer took a pitch, then he lined one down the short left-field line. He thought it might go foul, but it stayed fair and was long enough to reach the lower-deck seats for a grand slam that vaulted the Cardinals into a 4–3 lead. Sitting not far from where it landed was Whitey Kurowski, the Cardinals third baseman on the 1942 team whose home run in the ninth inning of that year's fifth game to nearly the same spot, had sealed the Cardinals Series victory.

Almost as happy as Boyer, though, was Eddie Hession, a young accountant from Lowell, Massachusetts, and big Kenny Boyer fan. Hession's sportswriter father had gotten his son and girlfriend tickets for the Saturday and Sunday games. Hession reached for the home run as it came at him in the left-field stands, got his mitt on it, then ripped his pants as he dove for the loose ball and smothered it on the concrete floor. Back at the hotel, the same one the Cardinals were staying at, Hession, his girlfriend, and Mr. and Mrs. Ken Boyer posed for a photo.

But long before that happy evening occasion, the Cardinals had to hold off the Yankees. Keane chose Ron Taylor to do that. Taylor, later a physician and team doctor for the Toronto Blue Jays, pitched four hitless and scoreless innings, walking—and stranding—only Mantle in the eighth. Keane commended Taylor for "challenging the hitters."

Game 5 was a rematch of the pitching pairing for the second game—Gibson vs. Stottlemyre. This time the "K" symbol appeared a lot on scorecards. Gibson fanned thirteen in ten innings while Stottlemyre struck out six in the seven frames he pitched. Gibson's opponents said his pitches were particularly overpowering in the fall afternoon shadows.

The game was scoreless until the Cardinals reached the tall Yankee right-hander for a pair of runs in the fifth. Gibson helped his own cause with a one-out single that fell in front of Tresh, who'd also had trouble judging a triple by Brock in the Series' first game. Flood then reached when Richardson took his eye momentarily off a ground ball, allowing both runners to reach safely. Brock drove home Gibson with a single to right, sending Flood to third. White drove in Flood with a ground-ball force play at second, with the Yankees hollering at first-base umpire Al Smith that they'd gotten White at first for a double play.

Gibson allowed only four hits and had eleven strikeouts entering the ninth. Mantle reached on an error by Groat to lead off the inning. Howard struck out. But Pepitone lined one viciously right back at Gibson, who deflected it toward the third-base line. Gibson pounced on it and, showing the acrobatics he'd once displayed as a member of the Harlem Globetrotters, fired an off-balance throw to White at first base. Umpire Smith shook his right fist vigorously signifying "out" as the Yankees accosted him to protest. Tresh followed with a four hundred-foot home run to right field, tying the score. (McCarver, in an interview for this book, said it's not a certainty that Tresh would have hit a home run if Pepitone had been called safe. And McCarver still believes the umpire got the call right.)

But the Cardinals came right back in the tenth off reliever Pete Mikkelsen. Bill White, 1–19 at that point, singled to lead off. Boyer tried to bunt him over and placed it so well that he beat it out for a hit. Groat tried to bunt both runners over but missed; Yankees catcher Elston Howard threw behind White trying to catch him going back to second, and White promptly darted for third base, making it with a head-first slide. Groat reached on a force play at second, White holding third. Up strolled Tim McCarver. The

Yankees' Berra said later that he didn't consider bringing in a left-hander to face the Cardinals catcher because Mikkelsen had a good slider that usually worked on portside swingers.

McCarver, four days shy of his twenty-third birthday, remembered that he had promised his mother back in Memphis that he would try to hit a homer for her. But when the belt-high fastball came in he was just trying to hit it far enough to get the lead runner in from third. It carried out well beyond the right-field wall and the Cardinals had a 5–2 lead. McCarver said he was "dazed" when he saw the ball go out, "happy" when he got to first base, and "laughing out loud" when he got to third. "I'm always laughing, even when I'm sad," he told the *Sporting News*. "The way I feel now, I'll never be sad again."

In the Yankees tenth, Gibson got pinch-hitter Mike Hegan to look at a called third strike, retired Linz on a harmless pop up, then gave a single to Richardson, who was nearing his own record of twelve hits in a Series. Maris followed by popping one foul near the VIP boxes just beyond the third-base dugout. Ken Boyer reached several rows into the stands, and just above a hunching NL president Warren Giles, to grab the ball and end the game.

More than 10,000 Cardinals fans met their heroes when they arrived at Lambert-St. Louis Municipal Airport that night. They fully expected the Cardinals, now leading three games to two, would wrap it up Wednesday.

Mid-seventies temperatures greeted the Cardinals as they took the field for Game 6. The first-inning pitching of Curt Simmons certainly revved up the crowd. With one on and one out, Simmons fanned both of the Yankees' M&M boys—Maris and Mantle—to end the inning. Curt Flood and Lou Brock greeted Jim Bouton with singles, putting runners on the corners for Bill White. He grounded into a double play, but it got the run home to give the Cardinals a 1–0 lead.

Simmons pitched the first four innings as if that slender lead might be enough, retiring the side in order in the second and third then keeping Richardson at first after he had led off the fourth with a single. The Cardinals middle of the order continued to struggle while McCarver got two hits and Simmons one during those same innings; but they too were left stranded.

In the Yankees fifth Tresh led off with a drive that the left-field-line umpire ruled fair but which Brock thought was foul after he had dived unsuccessfully for it. It bounded into the stands for a ground-rule double. Bouton singled in the run with two out from third to tie the game, thus repeating what Simmons had done to him by getting an RBI in the third game.

After White stranded two more runners with two out in the home half of the inning, the Yankees flexed their trademark home-run muscles in their sixth. With one out and no one on, Maris hit a hanging curveball just fair but far onto the pavilion roof in right field for a tie-breaker. On the next pitch, Mantle, batting right-handed, took an outside fastball to the pavilion roof to make it 3–1.

After Simmons left for a pinch-hitter in the 1–2–3 home half of the seventh, the Yankees put the game away against Barney Schultz, struggling in the Series after his brilliant regular season, and Gordie Richardson. Schultz gave up a two-out RBI single to Elston Howard then walked Tresh to load the bases. Keane brought in lefty Richardson to face Pepitone, who drove one to the pavilion roof for a grand slam and an insurmountable 8–1 lead that deflated the once-bubbling spectators.

Bouton's cap fell off only a dozen times in this start, and he needed relief help from six-foot, six-inch Steve Hamilton in the ninth. Berra put his hands well above his head in signaling for his reliever to signify that he wanted "the tall one."

Berra had said throughout the Series that Ford had a heel that was painful to land on, which is why he wasn't pitching. But New York sportswriter Dick Young broke the story that Ford actually had arm trouble. It was later determined to be blood circulation problems in his left arm. The stage was now set for a Gibson-Stottlemyre rematch in Game 7, both starters coming back on two days rest.

A crowd of 30,346 went through the turnstiles, with standing-room and bleacher tickets still available at the outset of the contest. Though not as sharp as on Monday, Gibson shut out the Yankees over the first four innings while Stottlemyre kept the Cardinals from scoring in the first three frames.

That changed in the home half of the fourth. Boyer led off with a single to center and moved up on a walk to Groat. Boyer scored when McCarver rapped to Pepitone, who forced Groat at second; but McCarver reached on an errant return throw by Linz. Shannon followed with a single, moving McCarver to third. With Maxvill at bat, the Cardinals successfully pulled off a delayed double steal, Shannon disrupting Richardson's return throw to home, which allowed McCarver to slide in safely. When Maxvill singled to right, Coach Vern Benson waved Shannon home, taking advantage of Mantle's injured right shoulder and giving the Cardinals a 3–0 lead they took into the fifth.

After Gibson got out of a two-on, one-out jam via a double play, Al Downing came on to pitch for the Yankees. Leading off, Brock greeted his fellow left-handed thrower with a home run deep to the pavilion roof. White found his lost hitting stroke and banged a single to right. Boyer demonstrated that he truly was back in the groove by doubling to right-center, moving White to third, from where he scored on a ground out. Boyer went to third and came home on a sacrifice fly by McCarver.

Overconfident Cardinals fans, however, were reminded that the Yankees were still a team of pride and prowess. Richardson began the sixth with a single, a record thirteenth hit that broke Pepper Martin's 1931 mark of twelve Richardson had tied in 1960. Maris poked a single to right. Then Mantle, batting left-handed, went to the opposite field, as he had the day before, putting a pitch by Gibson deep into the left-center-field bleachers to cut the lead to 6–3.

Gibson was on the ropes. Keane visited and asked if he still had his stuff, telling the big Cardinals right-hander that he'd give him one more batter. Gibson rared back and struck out Howard. After a pop-fly out and a walk, he fanned Clete Boyer to end the inning.

Gibson struck out one in each of the next two innings while keeping the Yankees from scoring. In the home half of the seventh, captain Kenny Boyer belted a two-out solo homer off Steve Hamilton to give Gibson and the Cardinals a little more breathing room.

They'd need it. In the ninth, with a frenzied Cardinals crowd providing a defeaning chorus, Gibson struck out Tom Tresh to lead off the inning. But he gave up a homer to Clete Boyer, the next hitter. He fanned pinch-hitter Johnny Blanchard for his thirty-first strikeout, a Series record he would break with thirty-five in 1968. But Phil Linz then homered to left and Bobby Richardson walked to the plate while Roger Maris, as the potential tying run, went to the on-deck circle. Keane, who'd had several relievers warming up, stuck with Gibson to finish the game. "I made a commitment to his heart," the manager would say later.

Richardson popped up near second base. Maxvill caught it and an exhausted Gibson nearly fell into the arms of third baseman Kenny Boyer as the celebration began.

Newspapers ran a photo of a happy Gussie Busch with a bear hug around an uncomfortable-looking Johnny Keane in the victors' clubhouse. The Big Eagle called a press conference for the next day to announce a new contract for the Cardinals manager. But when Keane showed up late for the event, he gave an impatient Busch a letter, announcing his resignation. On that same day the Yankees fired Berra, who had expected to be rehired. Days later

Keane signed on as the Yankees manager for 1965.

The Cardinals hired Cardinal legend Red Schoendienst as their new manager. But the magic of 1964 wasn't there the next season, and the team tumbled to seventh place. White, Boyer, and Groat were traded at season's end. Sadecki was 6–15 and dealt the following year. After one more good year in 1965, Barney Schultz became a minor-league coach. The Cardinals, however, would retool and earn another World Series ring just two years later.

The *Sporting News*, however, named Keane manager of the year in 1964. Devine's fellow major-league general managers voted him executive of the year. Three years later Busch would rehire him as general manager.

1964 Line Scores

Game 1, Wednesday, October 7, at Busch Stadium, St. Louis

	1 2 3 4 5 6 7 8 9	R	H	E
New York	0 3 0 0 1 0 0 1 0	5	12	2
St. Louis	1 1 0 0 0 4 0 3 x	9	12	0

W—Sadecki L—Ford

Time—2:42 Attendance—30,805

Summary: Mike Shannon's moon shot off bleachers scoreboard woke up Redbirds' offense in sixth-inning uprising while Barney Schultz kept Yankees at bay over last three frames.

Game 2, Thursday, October 8, at Busch Stadium

	1 2 3 4 5 6 7 8 9	R	H	E
New York	0 0 0 1 0 1 2 0 4	8	12	0
St. Louis	0 0 1 0 0 0 0 1 1	3	7	0

W—Stottlemyre L—Gibson

Time—2:29 Attendance—30,805

Summary: Disputed hit batsman call in sixth allowed Yankees to take lead while Mel Stottlemyre stymied Cardinals offense.

Game 3, Saturday, October 10, at Yankee Stadium, New York

	1 2 3 4 5 6 7 8 9	R	H	E
St. Louis	0 0 0 0 1 0 0 0 0	1	6	0
New York	0 1 0 0 0 0 0 0 1	2	5	2

W—Bouton L—Schultz

Time—2:16 Attendance—67,101

Summary: Mickey Mantle avoided goat's horns from earlier error by hitting upper-deck homer off Schultz to give Yankees 2–1 Series lead.

Game 4, Sunday, October 11, at Yankee Stadium

	1 2 3 4 5 6 7 8 9	R	H	E
St. Louis	0 0 0 0 0 4 0 0 0	4	6	1
New York	3 0 0 0 0 0 0 0 0	3	6	1

W—Craig L—Downing
Time—2:18 Attendance—66,312

Summary: Ken Boyer hit Al Downing's only bad pitch for a grand slam, and two Cardinals relievers shut down Yankees batters as Cardinals knotted Series.

Game 5, Monday, October 12, at Yankee Stadium

	1 2 3 4 5 6 7 8 9 10	R	H	E
St. Louis	0 0 0 0 2 0 0 0 0 3	5	10	1
New York	0 0 0 0 0 0 0 0 2 0	2	6	2

W—Gibson L—Mikkelsen
Time—2:37 Attendance—65,633

Summary: Tim McCarver's three-run homer in tenth gave Cardinals win and Series lead. Tom Tresh's two-out, two-run homer tied the game in the ninth.

Game 6, Wednesday, October 14, at Busch Stadium

	1 2 3 4 5 6 7 8 9	R	H	E
New York	0 0 0 0 1 2 0 5 0	8	10	0
St. Louis	1 0 0 0 0 0 0 1 1	3	10	1

W—Bouton L—Simmons
Time—2:37 Attendance—30,805

Summary: Yankees used their legendary home run power to even Series as Jim Bouton again turned in a strong performance on mound.

Game 7, Thursday, October 15, at Busch Stadium

	1	2	3	4	5	6	7	8	9	R	H	E
New York	0	0	0	0	0	3	0	0	2	5	9	2
St. Louis	0	0	0	3	3	0	1	0	x	7	10	1

W—Gibson L—Stottlemyre

Time—2:40 Attendance—30,346

Summary: Slumbering Cardinals bats of Bill White and Boyer awakened with a vengeance, while tired Gibson pitched complete game on guts and heart. Mantle showed greatness one more time in pulling Yankees close, but Cardinals held off last-inning rally to capture crown.

Total attendance: 321,807
Total receipts: $2,243,187.96
Cardinals player's share: $8,622.19

1967

Cardinals Defeat Red Sox 4 Games to 3

GAME 1:	CARDINALS	2	RED SOX	1
GAME 2:	CARDINALS	0	RED SOX	5
GAME 3:	CARDINALS	5	RED SOX	2
GAME 4:	CARDINALS	6	RED SOX	0
GAME 5:	CARDINALS	1	RED SOX	3
GAME 6:	CARDINALS	4	RED SOX	8
GAME 7:	CARDINALS	7	RED SOX	2

REGULAR-SEASON STARTING LINEUP		
Lou Brock	lf	NL-leading 113 runs, 52 steals
Curt Flood	cf	.335
Roger Maris	rf	18 game-winning RBIs
Orlando Cepeda	1b	111 RBIs, NL MVP
Tim McCarver	c	.295, MVP runner-up
Mike Shannon	3b	77 RBIs
Julian Javier	2b	.281, 14 HR
Dal Maxvill	ss	second in assists for NL SSs

PITCHERS		
Bob Gibson	13-7	missed nearly 8 weeks
Dick Hughes	16-6	29-year-old rookie
Nelson Briles	14-5	won last 9 decisions
Steve Carlton	14-9	168 Ks
Ray Washburn	10-7	3.53 ERA
Larry Jaster	9-7	3.02 ERA

BENCH	
Phil Gagliano	inf
Ed Spiezio	inf
Alex Johnson	of
Bobby Tolan	of

How the Cardinals Got to the World Series:

After two consecutive second-division finishes, the Cardinals unexpectedly won the National League pennant easily, finishing with a 101–60 record and a 10½-game lead. First baseman Orlando Cepeda led the league in RBIs and was the first-ever unanimous choice in the NL's Most Valuable Player balloting. Although ace Bob Gibson missed more than seven weeks with a broken leg, the Cardinals had outstanding pitching depth, with seven hurlers winning nine or more games.

The Cardinals' Series Opponent:

After finishing ninth in a ten-team league in 1966, the Boston Red Sox shocked the baseball world by winning the American League championship in 1967 under rookie manager Dick Williams. The pennant race was one of the tightest and most dramatic in history, with four clubs battling to the wire before Boston won out on the final day of the schedule. Carl Yastrzemski enjoyed a superb MVP season winning the American League triple crown with 44 homers, 121 RBIs, and a .326 average. The Red Sox also had other young hitters just coming into their own, notably George Scott, Reggie Smith, and Rico Petrocelli. Boston's pitching featured AL Cy Young Award winner Jim Lonborg, who finished 22–9. The rest of the staff, however, was average at best.

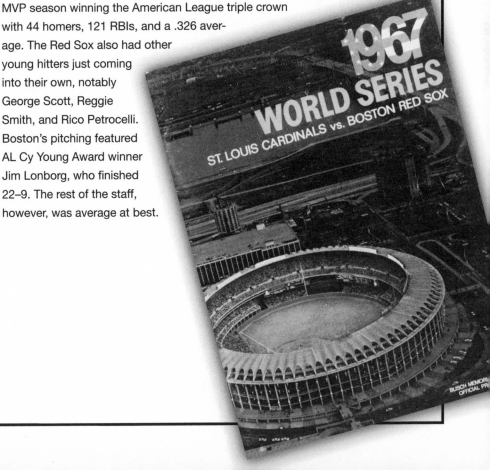

1967
WORLD SERIES
ST. LOUIS CARDINALS vs. BOSTON RED SOX

El Birdos and Champagne, Cha Cha Cha

The Cardinals woke up on the morning of World Series Game 7 in Quincy, Massachusetts, in a suburban motel with no room service, no real restaurant. No respect. The Boston media, meanwhile, was gushing over the chance for a World Championship by their "Impossible Dream" Red Sox. Sox manager Dick Williams was headlined in one newspaper as predicting, "It'll be Lonborg and Then Champagne." No respect. On the way to the park, Cardinals pitcher Bob Gibson confessed that he hadn't had any breakfast. St. Louis sportswriter Bob Broeg had to jump off the team bus to bring the hurler two fried egg sandwiches in the clubhouse. The Redbird ace had beaten the Red Sox twice already in this Series, but Boston first baseman George Scott was saying in another headline that, "We'll KO Gibson in Five." No respect. The Cardinals reached the ballpark determined to teach Boston some respect.

In a preseason poll of sportswriters, the Cardinals had been given very little respect. Of the 255 writers surveyed, only 16 had picked the Cardinals to win the National League pennant, with the consensus consigning St. Louis to sixth place. Since taking over as manager after the abrupt departure of Johnny Keane following the 1964 World Series, Red Schoendienst had led the team to seventh place in 1965 and sixth in 1966. A ten-time All Star as a player, Red believed in keeping the game uncomplicated and letting his players utilize their own strong points. In 1967, however, he made a couple of key moves. After the Cardinals acquired veteran right fielder Roger Maris, Schoendienst asked incumbent outfielder Mike Shannon to shift to third base. The twenty-seven-year-old Shannon worked out laboriously over the winter and through the spring to become an adequate third sacker, enabling the Cardinals to have both him and Maris in the lineup together. Red's other critical decision was the use a five-man pitching rotation. No National League champion had ever had five regular starters, but Redbird ace Bob Gibson urged the move to aid his aching elbow, and Schoendienst was confident his other pitchers could take up the slack. Dick Hughes, a twenty-nine-year-old rookie, stepped up and would wind up the team's top winner. The team was the surprise leader in the NL race by late June and held a 3½-game lead at the All Star Game.

The biggest star on the team was first baseman and cleanup hitter Orlando Cepeda, who was leading the league with a .360 average at the break. A native of Puerto Rico, he was nicknamed "Cha Cha" for his fondness for Latin rhythms and his zest for life. His infectious personality helped make the Cardinals cast of characters a close-knit, fun-loving bunch. Coach Joe Schultz coined the term "El Birdos," the team adopted the moniker with gusto, and Cardinal mania swept the area and fueled record-setting attendance.

But just four games into the second half of the season the Cardinals suffered what many thought would be a fatal blow. Gibson was hit on the leg by a line drive off the bat of Roberto Clemente, cracking his right fibula. Shrugging off the pain, Gibby pitched to three more hitters before the bone snapped. He would be out for more than seven weeks. St. Louis's league lead quickly evaporated as Chicago moved into a first-place tie. But on July 25 the Cardinals regained sole possession of the lead with a dramatic 4–3 win over the Cubs, the game ending on a relay by second baseman Julian Javier to catcher Tim McCarver for a tag out at the home plate. The next day Gibson's replacement in the rotation, Nelson Briles, got his first win as a starter, and the Cardinals juggernaut was never headed again. By August 19 their lead was more than ten games, and the pennant was clinched with two weeks left on the schedule.

Around the country St. Louis was rated a solid favorite to win the World Series. But you would hardly know it in Boston as the Series opened. Red Sox star Carl Yastrzemski acknowledged that the Cardinals were "a good club. They've got everything, speed, hitting, pitching, and defense." But he predicted that the Sox would win the title in six games. Boston manager Dick Williams, citing his team's momentum from winning the pennant on the final day, said his team would win it in five.

One obvious disadvantage of clinching on the final day was that Boston's ace pitcher, Jim Lonborg, who had pitched the final game on Sunday, would not be able to start in Game 1 on Wednesday. The Cardinals pitching was well rested, with Gibson ready to start on his normal four days of rest. Instead of Lonborg, the Sox would use Jose Santiago, who had won four games in the final two weeks of the pennant race, two in relief and two as a starter.

Redbird leadoff hitter Lou Brock quickly set the tone for the Series in the top of the first by singling and stealing second base. Curt Flood struck out and Roger Maris walked, but cleanup man Orlando Cepeda's sharp hopper was turned into an inning-ending double play. The Cards loaded the bases in the second, but were foiled by another double-play grounder, this one off the bat of Gibson. Brock was at it again in the third, lining a single to center. Flood came through with a double down the left-field line, sending Brock to third. The Red Sox played the infield back, conceding a run, and Maris's bouncer to first base allowed Brock to score the first run of the classic.

Gibson, meanwhile, struck out five on the first eight Boston batters. Then Santiago shocked the world and shook the Fenway

Park rafters by jumping on a hanging curveball and hitting it over the Green Monster in left for a game-tying home run.

Brock kept the pressure on in the fourth, bouncing a two-out single to left with Julian Javier on second. Javier rounded third but was cut down at home on a beautiful throw by Yastrzemski.

The 1-1 tie lasted until the seventh when Brock (who else?) led off with a hard shot to right, his fourth single of the day. Lou quickly took off for second and dove in under the shortstop's tag for a stolen base. Flood neatly moved him to third with a bouncer to first base. With the infield in close this time, Maris rapped one toward the hole in the right side. Sox second sacker Jerry Adair was able to make a diving stop and throw the batter out, but Brock ran home unmolested with the go-ahead run.

That was all Gibson needed. Though he allowed a man to reach first in each of the final three innings, no one got to second, and the Cardinals fireballer finished with a six-hit, one-walk, ten-strike out, complete game, 2–1 victory.

In Thursday's Game 2, it would be Lonborg's turn to dominate. Mixing brushback fastballs with sliders on the outside corner, the six-foot, six-inch right-hander stopped the Cardinals cold, retiring the first nineteen men he faced. Flood finally broke the string by working a walk with one out in the seventh inning. Lonborg's no-hitter remained intact until two were out in the eighth, when Javier lined a high slider into the left-field corner for a double. In all, Lonborg allowed just the one walk and the one hit.

The offense was largely supplied by the other Boston superstar, Carl Yastrzemski. Leading off the fourth inning against Cardinal starter Dick Hughes, he tomahawked an inside fastball into the seats in right field for a home run. The Sox chased Hughes and added a run in the sixth on a pair of walks, an error on a bunt, and a sacrifice fly. Yaz then capped the scoring in the seventh inning with a long, three-run blast over the bullpen in right center off lefty reliever Joe Hoerner. The final score was Boston 5, St. Louis 0.

The Cardinal veterans were peeved at Lonborg's successful intimidation and were determined to square things away when the Series moved to St. Louis for Game 3. St. Louis starting pitcher Nelson Briles got right down to business by hitting Yastrzemski in the leg with a pitch in the first inning. Red Sox skipper Williams was livid, and umpire Frank Umont ordered both managers to cut out the brushbacks. Yaz was thrown out trying to advance on a short passed ball. Then Brock boomed a triple off the left-center-field wall and trotted home on a hit to center by Flood. The Cardinals were in control of the game and the World Series thereafter, as it turned out.

Mike Shannon picked on a high curve in the second inning for a two-run homer, effectively ending Red Sox starting pitcher Gary Bell's day. Brock would torment the losers for another run in the sixth, beating out a bunt, racing to third on a wild pickoff throw, and scoring on a single by Maris. And in the eighth Orlando Cepeda's two-out double plated Maris. (It would be Cepeda's only RBI of the Series, which he would finish with a measly .105 batting average.)

Although Briles was reached for leadoff hits in four innings, he escaped trouble until the Sox scored on two hits around a sacrifice in the sixth. A leadoff home run in the seventh by Reggie Smith was the only other damage against him. And, most significantly, he retired Yastrzemski on easy grounders each time after the hit-by-pitch.

For Sunday's Game 4, Schoendienst chose Gibson to pitch on three days of rest. Though the season plan had been to rest the starters for four days, Red thought his ace would be strong, since he had missed seven weeks with a broken leg and had shown no signs of fatigue in his six starts since returning to the rotation. Indeed, through the first half of the game Gibson pitched with surgical precision, pinpointing his sliders to get strikeouts and easy grounders. By that time the game was well in hand.

After being frustrated by Santiago in the first game, the Redbirds jumped all over the Puerto Rican right-hander in the fourth game, scoring four runs on six hits in the first inning. Brock led off with a topper to third that Dalton Jones could not handle, and Flood followed with a liner through the hole to left. Maris then stepped into an outside fastball and looped it just fair down into the left-field corner, allowing both runners to race home. Maris moved to third on a fly out and scored on a single by Tim McCarver. After an out and an infield hit, Dal Maxvill smacked a single to left to plate the fourth run of the inning.

Doubles by Cepeda and Javier enabled St. Louis to add two more runs in the third inning.

Gibson tired a little in the late going, allowing one baserunner in each of the final four innings, but he finished with a five-hit, one-walk shutout. The 6–0 win gave the Cardinals a commanding three-games-to-one lead in the World Series.

Now all the Cardinals had to do to win the championship in front of their home fans was to beat Lonborg in Game 5. It was not to be. Relying more on his fastball than in Game 2, the Stanford graduate again held the St. Louis bats nearly silent, pitching a three-hitter while walking no one. Lanky left-hander Steve Carlton pitched well for the home team giving up just three hits and two walks in six innings, but he took the loss thanks to an unearned run. Boston scored in the third inning after Joe Foy singled with one out. An error by Shannon on Mike Andrews's bunt put men on first and second. Carlton got the dangerous Yastrzemski to look at a third strike. But Ken Harrelson's ground ball snuck through the left side, and Foy was able to score.

Reliever Ron Willis gave up a walk, a double, and an intentional walk to open the Boston ninth and was replaced by Jack Lamabe. A bloop single by Elston Howard brought home one runner, and another man scored when Maris's throw to the plate sailed over the catcher. Maris spoiled Lonborg's bid for a second shutout with a two-out home run the bottom of the ninth. But Boston had won,

3–1, and had lived to fight another day, at least.

The Series resumed in Boston on Wednesday, October 11, with Gary Waslewski pitching for the home team. Having spent much of the season in the minor leagues, Waslewski had not started for the Sox since July 29. But he had pitched three hitless innings in relief in Game 3, so he was Williams's desperation choice. Dick Hughes, the Cardinals' top regular-season winner, would try to clinch the title for the visitors.

Boston broke on top, Rico Petrocelli lofting a home run into the net above the left-field wall in the second inning. But St. Louis quickly went ahead 2–1 in the third inning, Brock doing the damage with a two-out, RBI single, a stolen base, and a great headfirst slide across the plate following a single by Flood. Hughes, however, could not hold the lead. In the fourth inning Yastrzemski, Smith, and Petrocelli all hit solo homers to put the Sox ahead 4–2.

Waslewski was removed after walking two men in the sixth inning, but John Wyatt pitched out of the jam. In the seventh, however, Wyatt served up a two-run gopher ball to that man Brock, a 450-foot shot deep into the Fenway bleachers, tying the game at 4–4.

But the Red Sox bounced right back and cinched the game with six hits and four runs in the bottom of the seventh. Joe Foy's double over Brock's head and off the left-field wall broke the tie, and it took the Cardinals four pitchers to get through the inning. Gary Bell closed out the win for Boston with two scoreless innings, and the 8–4 verdict tied the Series at three games apiece.

So it would all come down to Game 7 and the ultimate pitching matchup: Gibson vs. Lonborg. Boston's ace was coming back with just two days rest, while Gibson had three days. But, as Williams pointed out, each man would be working one day short of his normal rest. Bob Gibson saw the headline, "It'll be Lonborg, and then Champagne," and, fortified with just one greasy-spoon egg sandwich for breakfast, set himself to the task. All of his teammates did as well. "No excuses, no reasons, nothing," is how Nelson Briles later recalled it, "That's what it is. Let's deal with it. Let's do it."

And do it they did. After two quick, scoreless innings for both sides, Dal Maxvill led off the Cardinal third. Maxie, the 152-pound weakling in the St. Louis batting order, pumped a long drive off the center field wall for a triple. Gibson then ripped a Lonborg pitch toward left, but it was snared by the third baseman. Brock, for once, failed to deliver, popping out. But Flood came to the rescue with a whistling single to center, giving St. Louis the lead. When Maris bounced a hit just past the first baseman, Flood motored to third. And when Lonborg bounced a curve to Cepeda, Flood raced home on the wild pitch.

Gibson blew away Boston in the third and fourth, striking out four of six hitters. Then he came to bat in the top of the fifth and mashed a towering drive off the wall but above the bleachers in center field for a home run. Up next, the best Brock could do was a pop fly single. But Lou turned it into a run by stealing both second and third and scoring on a long fly by Maris. Gibson and the Cards now had a commanding 4–0 lead.

Red Sox fans got their one brief moment to cheer in the bottom of the fifth. George Scott, first up, bashed one off the center-field wall. Flood could not corral the rebound right away, and Javier's relay to third was wild, allowing Scott to circle the bases on a triple and an error. Gibson had challenged him with his best fastball, and Scott had gotten it. After the game, the Red Sox first baseman, who had predicted that his teammates would knock Gibson out early, reflected on the pitcher's aggresiveness, "He'll never give in, he'll always challenge you. . . . That's what makes him a winner."

The cheering in Fenway was short lived. In the Cardinal sixth, McCarver's sinking liner was misplayed into a double, and Shannon's hot grounder was boxed around for an error. Williams came out to talk to Lonborg and decided to leave the tiring righty in. Four pitches later, Javier lifted a high fly over the wall for a three-run home run. St. Louis led 7–1 with the game just about over.

Gibson began to wear down in the last three innings, walking Yastrzemski in the seventh, giving up a double and a run to Petrocelli in the eighth, and a single to Yaz in the ninth. But a lightning 6–4–3 double play followed by a sweet strikeout of Scott ended the game as a 7–2 World Championship Victory.

Delirium soon overflowed the cramped visitors clubhouse at Fenway Park. As various dignitaries and reporters made statements and exchanged congratulations, the ballplayers paraded around jubilantly drinking to "Lonborg and Champagne, Cha, Cha, Cha." The bubbly flowed freely, and Bob Gibson's second fried egg sandwich was washed down with sparkling wine. How sweet it was to show them who's best!

Gibson had allowed just fourteen hits and three runs in three complete-game victories, and he was given the sports car by *Sport Magazine* for being the World Series MVP. Lou Brock, who had batted .414 with eight runs scored and seven stolen bases, was given a car by St. Louis radio station KMOX. The club turned down an invitation from President Lyndon Johnson to stop by the White House "for cocktails," heading right back to St. Louis instead for a long, happy party at Musial and Biggie's Restaurant.

The Cardinals had no trouble repeating as NL champions in 1968 but lost the World Series to the Detroit Tigers in seven games. Bob Gibson had a sensational 1.12 ERA to go with a 22–9 record, winning both the Cy Young and the MVP Awards and winning his first two starts in the World Series. But this time he and the Cardinals lost Game 7 to Mickey Lolich and the Tigers.

1967 Line Scores

Game 1—Wednesday, October 4, at Fenway Park, Boston

	1 2 3 4 5 6 7 8 9	R	H	E
St. Louis	0 0 1 0 0 0 1 0 0	2	10	0
Boston	0 0 1 0 0 0 0 0 0	1	6	0

W—Gibson L—Santiago
Time—2:22 Attendance—34,796

Summary: Bob Gibson allowed only one runner to get past second base, while Lou Brock had four singles, two stolen bases, and two runs scored, counting twice on infield outs by Roger Maris. Jose Santiago kept the Cardinals at bay most of the game and even provided the Boston offense with a home run.

Game 2—Thursday, October 5, at Fenway Park

	1 2 3 4 5 6 7 8 9	R	H	E
St. Louis	0 0 0 0 0 0 0 0 0	0	1	1
Boston	0 0 0 1 0 1 3 0 x	5	9	0

W—Lonborg L—Hughes
Time—2:24 Attendance—35,188

Summary: Jim Lonborg dominated the Cardinals hitters, allowing only a walk in the seventh inning and a double in the eighth. Carl Yastrzemski led the hitting with a solo homer in the fourth and a three-run blast in the seventh.

Game 3—Saturday, October 7, at Busch Memorial Stadium, St. Louis

	1 2 3 4 5 6 7 8 9	R	H	E
Boston	0 0 0 0 0 1 1 0 0	2	7	1
St. Louis	1 2 0 0 0 1 0 1 x	5	10	0

W—Briles L—Bell
Time—2:15 Attendance—54,575

Summary: Nelson Briles plunked Yastrezemski on the leg in the first inning and held him hitless thereafter. Brock tripled and scored in the bottom of the first, and Mike Shannon added a two-run homer in the second.

Game 4—Sunday, October 8, at Busch Memorial Stadium

	1 2 3 4 5 6 7 8 9	R	H	E
Boston	0 0 0 0 0 0 0 0 0	0	5	0
St. Louis	4 0 2 0 0 0 0 0 x	6	9	0

W—Gibson L—Santiago
Time—2:05 Attendance—54,575

Summary: Gibson was brilliant again, allowing only one runner past first base. The Cards kayoed Santiago with six hits in the first inning. Maris's two-run opposite field double opening the scoring.

Game 5—Monday, October 9, at Busch Memorial Stadium

	1 2 3 4 5 6 7 8 9	R	H	E
Boston	0 0 1 0 0 0 0 0 2	3	6	1
St. Louis	0 0 0 0 0 0 0 0 1	1	3	2

W—Lonborg L—Carlton

Time—2:20 Attendance—54,575

Summary: Lonborg was again dominant, walking none and allowing only two singles and a last-out home run in the ninth inning. A fumble by Shannon on a bunt set up the first Boston run, and a wild throw by Maris enabled Boston to add an insurance run.

Game 6—Wednesday, October 10, at Fenway Park

	1 2 3 4 5 6 7 8 9	R	H	E
St. Louis	0 0 2 0 0 0 2 0 0	4	8	0
Boston	0 1 0 3 0 0 4 0 x	8	12	1

W— Wyatt L—Lamabe

Time—2:48 Attendance—35,188

Summary: The Sox routed Dick Hughes with four solo homers in the first four innings. Brock's two-run home run tied the game in the top of the seventh. But six hits in the bottom of the round won the game for Boston, with Joe Foy's double off the left-field wall driving in the tie-breaking run.

Game 7—Thursday, October 12, at Fenway Park

	1 2 3 4 5 6 7 8 9	R	H	E
St. Louis	0 0 2 0 2 3 0 0 0	7	10	1
Boston	0 0 0 0 1 0 0 1 0	2	3	1

Winning—Gibson L—Lonborg

Time—2:23 Attendance—35,188

Summary: The Cardinals finally got to Lonborg for seven runs in six innings, while Gibson stopped the Red Sox on three hits. Dal Maxvill's booming triple opened the third-inning rally, Gibson added a solo homer in the fifth, and Julian Javier clinched the verdict with a three-run bomb in the sixth.

Total attendance: 304,085

Total gate receipts: $2,350,607.10

Cardinals player's share: $8,314.81

1982

Cardinals Defeat Brewers 4 Games to 3

GAME 1:	**CARDINALS**	**0**	**BREWERS**	**10**
GAME 2:	**CARDINALS**	**5**	**BREWERS**	**4**
GAME 3:	**CARDINALS**	**6**	**BREWERS**	**2**
GAME 4:	**CARDINALS**	**5**	**BREWERS**	**7**
GAME 5:	**CARDINALS**	**4**	**BREWERS**	**6**
GAME 6:	**CARDINALS**	**13**	**BREWERS**	**1**
GAME 7:	**CARDINALS**	**6**	**BREWERS**	**3**

REGULAR-SEASON STARTING LINEUP		
Tommy Herr	2b	83 runs, 25 steals
Lonnie Smith	lf	68 stolen bases
Keith Hernandez	1b	.299, Gold Glove
George Hendrick	rf	19 HRs, 104 RBIs
Darrell Porter	c	.231, 48 RBIs
Willie McGee	cf	.296 as rookie
Ken Oberkfell	3b	led NL 3b in fielding
Ozzie Smith	ss	Gold Glove, 25 steals

PITCHERS		
Joaquin Andujar	15-10	5 shutouts, 2.47 ERA
Bob Forsch	15-9	3.48 ERA
Steve Mura	12-11	did not pitch in postseason
John Stuper	9-7	3.36 ERA as rookie
Bruce Sutter	9-8	league-leading 36 saves
Jim Kaat	5-3	62 games, age 43

BENCH	
Mike Ramsey	inf
Dane Iorg	of
David Green	of
Gene Tenace	c

How the Cardinals Got to the World Series:

Fulfilling Manager Whitey Herzog's two-year rebuilding plan, the Cardinals won their first pennant in fourteen seasons. They played a brand of game called "Whiteyball," based on the manager's tailoring the team for cavernous Busch Stadium. It featured contact hitters with speed on the bases backed by air-tight defense, a dependable starting rotation, and a lights-out closer. The Redbirds vaulted into the Eastern Division lead with an early twelve-game winning streak then held off the Philadelphia Phillies' challenge in September. The club was consistent throughout the year, winning the same number of games at home as on the road and completing the season with a 92–70 record, finishing three games ahead of second-place Philadelphia. The Cardinals then swept the Atlanta Braves 3–0 in the National League Championship Series to claim the franchise's thirteenth pennant.

The Cardinals' Series Opponent:

The Milwaukee Brewers, nicknamed "Harvey's Wallbangers" for manager Harvey Kuenn and the team's league-leading 216 home runs, used a 26–8 surge shortly after Kuenn replaced fired manager Buck Rodgers in June to vault into the AL East lead at the All-Star break. The club featured three future Hall of Famers: shortstop Robin Yount, third baseman Paul Molitor, and ace reliever Rollie Fingers. The Brewers beat the Orioles on the season's final day to win the Eastern Division by a game with a 95–67 record. Milwaukee spotted the California Angels a 2–0 lead in the ALCS then took three straight to claim the pennant, the first for the Brewers and the first for Milwaukee since the Milwaukee Braves topped the NL in 1958.

Whiteyball versus Harvey's Wallbangers

Cardinals fans who believed in omens saw a bad one in the opening game of the 1982 World Series.

The Milwaukee Brewers not only humiliated the Redbirds 10–0 but also did so with plenty of singles, a style more in line with the Cardinals' usual attack method. Harvey's Wallbangers, as the powerful Brewers of manager Harvey Kuenn were called, hit only one home run, that by former Cardinal Ted Simmons. And Mike Caldwell, a pitcher whom the Cardinals had given up on after a brief spring training tryout a few years before, pitched the complete-game shutout.

But the Cardinals of Whitey Herzog had rallied several times during crucial moments of the 1982 season. They were about to do so again.

Many would say that Gussie Busch's June 1980 hiring of Whitey Herzog to manage the Cardinals was the finest move the beer baron made during his thirty-six years as team president. One longtime observer, Hall of Fame broadcaster Jack Buck, would later say over the airwaves that the new life Herzog brought to the franchise was a reason Buck decided to stay behind the mike after watching a frustrating decade of Cardinals baseball.

The Cardinals of the 1970s had their moments—though very few. The team finished second in the Eastern Division three times and contended in the early parts of two other seasons. But twice the Cardinals lost ninety or more games. In early 1980 they were going nowhere under Ken Boyer, the popular former MVP Cardinals third baseman who'd managed them for nearly two years.

Herzog, a New Athens, Illinois, native, had taken the Kansas City Royals to the bridesmaid's role in the American League Championship Series from 1976 through 1978, losing all three years to the New York Yankees. Fired after a second-place finish in 1979, Herzog accepted the Big Eagle's offer to run the Cardinals.

It was a match of focused, successful men who spoke their minds freely and honestly and who trusted each other implicitly from the start. When Busch asked Herzog for his assessment of the team, Herzog gave it to him straight: too slow, bad defensively, and lacking a winning attitude.

Busch allowed "The White Rat," as Herzog had been nicknamed early in his playing career because of his bleached-out shock of blond hair, to also act as general manager later that season. Herzog gave the Cardinals a major facelift. Over a five-day period in December 1980, he shipped thirteen Cardinals to three different teams in return for eight players.

In doing so, Herzog at first alienated many longtime Cardinals fans by trading to Milwaukee such favorites as catcher Ted Simmons, a perennial .300 hitter who supplied what little power those 1970s Cardinals teams had, and bulldog starting pitcher Pete Vuckovich. Both would help the Brewers become instant contenders in the AL East, as would ace reliever Rollie Fingers, whom Herzog had obtained for several days from the San Diego Padres only to include him in the Milwaukee deal. Herzog also discarded promising youngsters Terry Kennedy and Leon Durham, who would face each other in the 1984 NL playoffs, Kennedy on the Padres and Durham on the Chicago Cubs.

But it was the players Herzog got in return who would help him begin to mold the team he envisioned for spacious, Astroturf-covered Busch Stadium. Bruce Sutter from the Cubs would anchor the bullpen and save many a Cardinals victory from 1981 to 1984. Gene Tenace would be a steady backup catcher to Darrell Porter, whom Herzog signed as a free agent after having managed him on the Kansas City Royals. Dave LaPoint would steady the starting rotation.

The Cardinals had the best record in the NL East in 1981, but a players' strike cancelled the middle third of the season. The Cardinals watched the playoffs on TV because they hadn't won either the first- or second-half split seasons Major League Baseball declared to appease fans after the strike was settled.

Herzog continued building his team in the off-season, shipping troubled shortstop Garry Templeton along with outfielder Sixto Lezcano and pitcher Luis DeLeon to the Padres for fielding wizard Ozzie Smith and pitchers Steve Mura and Alan Olmstead. Getting outfielder Lonnie Smith from the Philadelphia Phillies in a three-team deal gave the Redbirds the good-hitting speedy leadoff man the team needed. The addition of Joaquin Andujar also helped solidify the rotation. And dealing pitcher Bob Shirley, one of the players gotten from San Diego in December 1980, to the Yankees for a minor leaguer named Willie McGee would pay dividends when the Cardinals needed an outfielder in May.

The Cardinals won twelve in a row beginning the second week of the 1982 season then fought off challenges first from the Montreal Expos then the Phillies in September. The consistent Cardinals never lost more than three in a row until after they'd clinched the divisional title. Veteran Bob Forsch and Andujar led the club with fifteen wins each while Sutter led the league with thirty-six saves.

Silent George Hendrick, who wouldn't talk to the media, led the team with nineteen homers, and only Porter would also reach double figures in that department, with twelve. Yet Tommy Herr, then in his first full season, and Ozzie Smith would become a formidable double-play combo, with Ken Oberkfell moving to third base. And Keith Hernandez, a holdover from the pre-Whitey days along with Hendrick, would help anchor the infield while holding down the important number-three spot in the batting order.

The Cardinals would hit only sixty-seven homers as a team, two of them inside the park, and Herzog would crack that he wondered during the year if the club would break Roger Maris's then-record of sixty-one. But this Redbird bunch, a rebirth of the St. Louis Swifties idea from the 1940s, led the league with two hundred stolen bases.

The Cardinals had an easy time with the Braves—managed by former Cardinals infielder and batting champ Joe Torre, with former Cardinals Bob Gibson and Dal Maxvill as coaches. The Cardinals swept Atlanta three straight after rain threatened to end the scheduled first game in a regulation five-innings with the Braves up 1–0. But the umps stopped the game with one out in the bottom of the fifth, and the rain never let up, causing a cancellation.

Cardinals players credited Herzog with maintaining a well-oiled machine. They said he made all twenty-five players feel they were a part of the club by explaining to each his role. They also said Herzog, like a good chess player, was always several plays—and even innings—ahead in his thinking. He would tell a player on the bench to be ready to come in if and when a particular situation arose later in the game. He said he got to know his players better by going fishing with them.

Never a star and rarely an everyday player during his eight-year career with four American League teams, Whitey developed his managing style by absorbing the good and disdaining the bad of the pilots he often sat near on the bench.

The Cardinals had had likeable managers over the years—Johnny Keane, Red Schoendienst, Ken Boyer. But the fans' support for the iconic Whitey Herzog went well beyond mere popularity. Their adulation continues to this day; his induction into the Hall of Fame in 2010 was celebrated by locals as Catholics would if a person from their parish were canonized. Herzog endeared himself to Cardinals fans because he came off as a down home guy who drank beer, liked fishing, and said what he believed. He was also dramatic on the field and persuasive in TV commercials he made for a variety of Cardinals sponsors.

Best of all, in two seasons at the helm, Herzog had made the Cardinals winners again.

While more than 53,000 Cardinals fans would fill Busch Stadium to standing-room only for each of the four games, TV viewers nationwide would help set a record at that time. Game 7 was viewed by an estimated 31.8 million households, a record for any baseball game.

It also would mark the Cardinals' first encounter with the American League's designated hitter. In the 1980s, the rules for World Series in even-numbered years allowed both teams to use it. Herzog would use four men at that offense-only position.

This Series promised a contrast in offensive styles between the Brewers, who banged the ball against or over the wall, and the Cardinals, who punched the ball down on the turf or through holes in the infield then rattled the pitcher and his defense by either stealing or threatening to do so. It was the first World Series to match the team who led the majors in home runs against the team with the fewest. One-time Cardinals favorites—catcher Ted Simmons and pitcher Pete Vuckovich—were now in the blue road uniforms of Milwaukee.

Both teams were good defensively and had dependable starting pitching. Both had future Hall of Famers as closers—the Cardinals' Bruce Sutter and the Brewers' Rollie Fingers. However, an ailing elbow kept Fingers out of the Series—he didn't pitch after September 2—though he donned his uniform for every game.

Pitching pairings for the first game, on Tuesday, October 12, at Busch Stadium, offered much hope for Redbird rooters. Their steadiest hurler over the previous few years, Bob Forsch, was starting. He'd pitched a three-hit, complete-game, 7–0 win over the Atlanta Braves in the first game of the NLCS. Always a good hitter, he'd even gotten two hits and an RBI in that one.

Never flashy, colorful, or controversial, the right-handed Forsch had been the definition of the journeyman, never missing a start and usually throwing more than two hundred innings a season. He'd won twenty games in 1977 and pitched a no-hitter the following year. While his regular-season lifetime record through 1982 was a modest 98–83, he'd never had an ERA in any season go over 3.94; in 1982 it had been a respectable 3.48.

His opponent was southpaw Mike Caldwell. At thirty-three, a year older than Forsch, he'd had a spring tryout with the Cardinals in 1977 but been traded to Cincinnati before the season and then to Milwaukee during that year. Like Forsch, he'd had twenty-win year, in 1978, and was a grind-it-out kind of guy. But, Cardinals fans noticed, Caldwell had lasted only three innings and given up five earned runs in the first game of the ALCS against the Angels, getting saddled with the loss.

But high expectations sometimes are quashed—and early—as happened to Cardinals rooters that night. "There was not a rewarding moment for the Cardinals at any time," venerable *St. Louis Globe-Democrat* sports editor Bob Burnes would write.

The Brewers scored two runs in the first in a manner the Cardinals often did during the season, by taking advantage of a walk, an error by usually reliable gloveman Keith Hernandez at first, and an infield single. Kuenn's musclemen went over the wall only once, when Simmons hit one out in the fifth. Of the Brewers' seventeen hits, thirteen were singles, again closer to the 75 percent margin of one-base hits the Cardinals had had during the season (about 67 percent of the Brewers' hits had been singles). Leadoff man Paul Molitor had a record five hits, retired only the first time he batted. Shortstop Robin Yount, who batted second, had four safeties. Both would eventually be elected to the Hall of Fame. Forsch came out during the sixth inning, giving up ten hits and six runs, four earned.

The final was 10–0, one of the worst drubbings in World Series history. Busch Stadium was only about half filled in the later innings.

Trying to put a moment of humor afterwards, Herzog cracked, "I'm glad we weren't scheduled for a double-header." But he credited Caldwell. The Brewers' lefty gave up three hits and walked only one in pitching a complete game. Caldwell called it "my best pitching of the year."

Harvey Kuenn had grown up in a Milwaukee suburb and started his playing career in 1953 as a shortstop for the Detroit Tigers. By the end of the decade he'd moved to the outfield. Never a power hitter, Kuenn nevertheless was a solid contact hitter, leading the AL in hits four times and doubles three times in the 1950s. He captured the 1959 AL batting championship with a robust .353.

However, as a player he is too often remembered only for being involved in an unpopular trade with the Cleveland Indians for home run hitter Rocky Colavito right before the 1960 season. Kuenn played through Indians fans' unhappiness at losing their hero then went on to help the San Francisco Giants win the 1962 pennant. He played through 1966, finishing with a lifetime .303 batting average.

By the late 1970s he had befriended Milwaukee Brewers' owner Bud Selig and become a batting instructor for the team, earning the respect of many hitters. In June 1982 he finally got the chance to manage when the club fired Buck Rodgers with the Brewers 23–24. Kuenn told the players to relax and have fun. He used a set lineup from game to game. An ever-present tobacco chaw bulging out his cheek, he showed confidence in his pitchers. His players, in turn, patronized the Milwaukee tavern Kuenn and his wife Audrey operated, drinking Miller beer. The Brewers went 72–43 under Kuenn.

They nearly blew a four-game lead with five to play. But veteran Don Sutton, whom they'd acquired on August 30, beat the Orioles' Jim Palmer on the final day of the season, breaking a tie between the two clubs and giving Milwaukee its first first-place finish since the Braves had tied the Dodgers at the top of the NL standings in 1959. The Brewers then spotted the California Angels a 2–0 lead in games before winning the League Championship Series.

And with the same lineup he'd used for the opener, Kuenn gave the ball to Sutton to start the second game. Herzog countered with rookie John Stuper. Cardinals fans had to be concerned.

That was especially true when the Brewers took a 3–0 lead early. Right fielder Charley Moore doubled home a run in the second. Paul Molitor got his sixth hit of the Series leading off the third, stole second, and moved to third on a wild pitch, scoring on a ground out by Yount. One out later Simmons parked his second homer deep into the right-field bleachers.

But the Cardinals finally got on the scoreboard in their third, thanks to an RBI double by Tommy Herr and a run-scoring single by Ken Oberkfell. However, the Brewers knocked Stuper out in the fifth, adding a run to take a 4–2 lead, which Sutton protected as the Cardinals came to bat in the sixth.

With one out Oberkfell singled, stole second, moved to third on a fly out, then watched as George Hendrick walked. It was the Cardinals' second stolen base of the game, and Herzog later explained that his team had to run, regardless of the score. He said he been criticized that season by another manager for stealing a base when the Cardinals had been up by five runs; Herzog said he told his fellow manager that the Cardinals wouldn't run with a five-run lead if the other team would promise not to score any more.

Now with two on and two out, Cardinals catcher Darrell Porter walked to the plate. Cardinals fans have always given new players a chance, even those who replaced popular ones. Porter had joined the Royals in 1977 and played great baseball for Herzog in Kansas City after having five decent years for the Brewers. But he'd admitted to having drug problems, undergone therapy, and become a devout Christian. Two quiet seasons in St. Louis—.224 and .231—had not endeared him to those who still wished that Simmons was catching for the Cardinals, especially after Simmons hit home runs in each of the first two games. Sutton had the left-handed swinging Porter down one ball, two strikes when he threw a slider on the outside corner. Porter slashed it down the left-field line and into the corner, chasing home both runs and tying the game at four-all.

Porter told the press later, "I can't remember the last time I hit one to left. No, I wasn't trying to do it. But the slider stayed outside, and I went with it."

Herzog had never given up on his backstop. Perhaps with a touch of sarcasm, he noted the cheers that Porter's newfound fans had given him.

Rollie Fingers and Bruce Sutter were the prime relief pitchers in baseball then. Today each would be used only if his team had the lead entering the ninth. Then, however, both Sutter and Fingers were accustomed to relief stints of more than two innings. Sutter had had eight of them in 1982, Fingers ten.

With two out in the seventh, Cecil Cooper doubled. Sutter was summoned from the bullpen, becoming the Cardinals' fourth pitcher. He intentionally walked Simmons then got Ben Oglivie to ground out. Sutter gave up a two-out single in the eighth but stranded the runner.

In the Cardinals' half of the eighth, Keith Hernandez led off with a walk but was forced out at second by George Hendrick. Porter then lined a single to center, the runner stopping at second. That brought rookie right-hander Pete Ladd out of the Milwaukee bullpen.

Perhaps both Brewers and Cardinals fans could ask, "What if Fingers had come in?" On a three-two fastball, Ladd, many of the spectators, and perhaps even Lonnie Smith, thought the pitcher had caught the corner for a strikeout. "I saw Lonnie start toward the dugout then looking back at the umpire in surprise," Ladd said later, adding that he thought the pitch "got every bit of the plate." But AL umpire Bill Haller called it ball four, loading the bases. Herzog sent Steve Braun to pinch-hit for David Green; this time Ladd wasn't as close, and Braun walked on four pitches, forcing in the leading run.

Sutter gave a leadoff single to Molitor then saw Porter throw him out trying to steal. The next two men went down meekly, and the Cardinals won 5–4, tying the Series.

Numerous great hitting and great fielding displays have marked World Series contests. But rarely has one player put on as great an offensive and defensive show in the same game as did Cardinals center fielder Willie McGee in the third contest, at Milwaukee's County Stadium.

It marked the first time since 1958 that Milwaukee had hosted a World Series contest, when the Braves had met the Yankees. A rested but raring-to-go Pete Vuckovich started against an equally revved up Joaquin Andujar.

The night was chilly, but the "one tough Dominican," as Andujar called himself, wore only his jersey with no undershirt beneath it. He would later say that the weather never bothered him. His pitching bothered the Brewers, who went down in order in four of the first five innings. McGee aided by pulling down a long drive at the center field fence hit by leadoff man Molitor.

Meanwhile, the Cardinals were almost as futile against Vuckovich—until the fifth. With one out, Lonnie Smith, batting sixth, lined a double. Designated hitter Dane Iorg reached on an error. The switch-hitting McGee, batting left handed, then drove one deep into the right-field seats for 3–0 lead that would turn out to be one more than they needed to win.

However, in this Series, victory was never certain for either team after the opening game blowout.

Two innings later, Lonnie Smith would triple and score on a throwing error by the second baseman. One batter later McGee would crack another home run off Vuckovich, making it 5–0.

Andujar, cruising along with a two-hitter, retired the first batter in the seventh easily. But Simmons rifled one back through the box, hitting Andujar just below the right knee. He went down as if shot then dramatically rolled back and forth, allowing everyone to see his facial grimaces as his teammates carried him off the field. When Kaat and Doug Bair each gave up a runner, loading the bases with two out, Sutter was again summoned. He retired Charlie Moore on a foul popup to Oberkfell at third.

But in the eighth, Sutter showed that even bullpen deities sometimes walk among mortals. With two out he walked Yount then gave up a home run to Cooper. He would remain on earth in the ninth, only to be bailed out that night by someone operating on a higher plain.

With the Cardinals having picked up an unearned run in the ninth, Sutter had a 6–2 lead with three outs to go. With one on and none out, he faced Gorman Thomas, whose bat had been strangely silent thus far. Thomas took one of Sutter's pitches deep to left center, appearing to have enough height to clear the fence. But McGee leaped higher than the wall and snared it. Sutter then struck out the next batter and induced Charley Moore to hit a fly ball that McGee had plenty of room to catch.

In this see-saw Series, the Cardinals were now on top, two games to one.

McGee was marking his first anniversary with the Cardinals, since he'd been traded to them by the Yankees during the 1981 World Series. He'd been bumped from the Yankees' forty-man off-season roster, and they decided to trade him for pitcher Bob Shirley rather than simply losing him in the draft. In the locker room after the game, McGee thanked Yankees owner George Steinbrenner for giving him the chance to play professional baseball. But he also said he was disappointed to learn about the trade well after the fact only through the newspapers and not directly from either team.

The always humble McGee, beloved by fans right from the start because of his shy appearance yet strong contributions to the team, also said he didn't appreciate being called "E.T." after the movie character.

Herzog said it publicly, but millions of fans thought it: "I don't know of anyone who played a better World Series game than he did tonight."

Players and experienced fans will tell you that bad hops and checked swings that result in hits are part of the game. Over a 162-game regular season they have a tendency to even out. But in a seven-game World Series they can be pivotal.

Entering the bottom of the seventh of the fourth game, Saturday, October 16, the Cardinals seemed headed toward another win and what could be an insurmountable three-games-to-one lead. They came out swinging and scoring. George Hendrick had driven in the first run in the opening inning with a two-out single. In the second, the Cardinals had gotten two runs on one sacrifice fly. McGee had singled with one out and stolen second, followed by a walk to Ozzie Smith. Both moved up on a wild pitch by Brewers starter Moose Haas. Tommy Herr followed with a fly ball to the warning track in center field; after a back-pedaling Gorman Thomas caught it, he lost his footing and fell backward, giving Smith enough time to scamper home after McGee. The Cardinals added another run that frame on a walk, stolen base, and error.

The teams then exchanged runs and the Redbirds took a 5–1 advantage into the home half of the seventh. Gorman Thomas started the inning harmlessly by fouling out to Porter. Ben Oglivie followed with what looked like a routine ground ball to Hernandez. But it took a big hop. "If it doesn't take the hop, I step on the bag myself," Hernandez said later. He tossed to pitcher Dave LaPoint, who'd come up through the Brewers' system.

LaPoint dropped the toss. Oglivie was safe. The Brewers took off.

Five hits, an unintentional walk, an intentional walk, a wild pitch—off LaPoint and the trio of ineffective relievers who followed—resulted in six runs. The most damaging hit was an "excuse me" checked swing by Yount with the bases loaded, two out, and the Cardinals still leading 5–2. Yount tried to hold up his swing on a high inside pitch from Doug Bair, but his bat still guided it into right field, plating two runs.

Bob McClure, who relieved in the eighth with the Cardinals rallying to put two on with one out, got McGee to hit into an inning-ending double play. He then retired the side in order in the ninth, striking out both Herr and pinch hitter Gene Tenace to end the game with the Brewers victorious 7–5 and the Series even.

Ordinarily a team getting fourteen hits off its opponent's starting pitcher has more than enough runs for a win. The Cardinals got that many off Mike Caldwell in Game 5, who wasn't as mesmerizing as he'd been in the opening contest.

But brilliant defensive plays by the Brewers' first, second, and third basemen as well as by their right fielder choked Cardinals rallies. Meanwhile Milwaukee again had no trouble measuring the pitches of Cardinals starter Bob Forsch.

As a result, the Cardinals spotted the Brewers a run in the first then spent the rest of the day playing catch-up. When they tied it 1–1 in the third, on a ringing RBI double by Hernandez, the Brewers came right back with a solo run on an RBI ground out by Cooper. Robin Yount, becoming the first man in Series history to have four hits in two games—in or out of a single Series—frustrated the Cardinals by hitting an opposite-field home run off Forsch in the seventh that made it 4–2. He did it to chants of "MVP, MVP" from the partisan Milwaukee crowd.

Herzog then brought Sutter in for the eighth to try to hold it close, but the Cardinals ace gave up two more runs on three hits and a walk.

Yet in the ninth, the Cardinals showed a spark of life that might have lifted their hopes and those of their fans. They finally chased Caldwell with consecutive doubles by David Green and Hernandez and an RBI single by Hendrick, with only one out. Bob McClure came on for the second straight day and gave up a single to Porter, sending Hendrick to second.

But McGee fanned. Gene Tenace then batted for Oberkfell, who had three hits and was hitting .323 for the Series, while Mike Ramsey pinch ran for Porter. Herzog later said he knew Oberkfell was hot but wanted Tenace in that situation since he had the better chance to hit a homer. He flied out to left, however, to end the game and send the Cardinals back to St. Louis and possible elimination.

Cardinals fans seeking an omen found a good one in the sixth game—despite the blustery conditions that had led to a tornado watch being issued.

On a wet Tuesday night, the Cardinals mauled the Brewers 13–1. The playing time was 2:21. The rain delays totaled more than two and a half hours.

Rookie John Stuper, who started the second game but didn't get the decision in the Cardinals' 5–4 win, again took the ball and again faced veteran Don Sutton.

This time it was no contest.

"It was a tour de force for the Cardinals, who had to win or be eliminated. And it was a tour de force for their rookie pitcher, John Stuper, who . . . stopped the leading offensive team in baseball on four hits," wrote the *New York Times*' Joseph Durso. Stuper took a shutout into the ninth and finished what he started.

Stuper retired the Brewers in order in the first and pitched out of a two-on, no-out jam in the second without giving up a run.

His teammates, with help from the Brewers' shaky defense this night, gave him all the runs he needed in the second when designated hitter Dane Iorg doubled down the left-field line with two out and scored when shortstop Robin Yount, the previous weekend's hero, booted a ground ball by Willie McGee. McGee then came around to the plate on a double by Tommy Herr.

They gave Stuper three more runs two innings later. Darrell Porter, swinging the hot bat that would earn him MVP honors in the Series, as it had in the NLCS, homered to right after George Hendrick had opened the frame with a single. Iorg then tripled, this time down the right-field line, and scored when squeezed home by a Herr bunt.

Stuper had faced the minimum over the previous two innings, aided by another double play in the third. Now in the fifth, with rain threatening, he needed to retire them to make the game official. World Series games had been postponed by rain, but no official game had ever been played in fewer than nine innings because of it.

"I was conscious of the rain, and I wanted to get them out as quick as possible in the fifth inning, but I wasn't going to be dumb about it," the Cardinals right-hander said afterward. "If I got a batter 0–2, I wasn't going to give him a pitch down the middle.'"

Stuper, twenty-five, a Pennsylvania native who went on to coach the Yale University baseball team, a job he still has, started in the Pittsburgh Pirates organization but came to the Cardinals in a 1979 trade. He made his major league debut in early June and gave the Cardinals nine wins against seven losses.

After Stuper retired the Brewers 1–2–3 in the fifth, Keith Hernandez hit a two-run homer in the Cardinals' half, making it 7–0. Jim Slaten was called in to relieve Sutton. Then the rains came and stopped play for twenty-six minutes.

In the sixth inning, Doc Medich replaced Slaton and absorbed a six-run uprising by the Cardinals, making it 13–0. The rally was interrupted by a two-hour-and-thirteen-minute rain delay.

Jim Kaat, oldest Cardinal player, warmed up alongside Stuper as play was about to resume—bullpens then were in foul territory down the left- and right-field lines. But Stuper returned. He said recently he wanted to finish the game to give the bullpen the night off. He also dedicated the game to his late father, "an outstanding amateur pitcher who never got to see me sign a pro contract." He lost his shutout in the ninth when Gantner led off with a double, moved to third on a soft hit by Molitor, and scored on a wild pitch.

The game ended at 12:21 a.m. But the wet fans who stayed were happy. The Series was tied three games each.

The omen: In the 1968 World Series the Tigers had returned to Busch Stadium for the sixth game trailing the Cardinals three games to two then had humiliated the Cardinals 13–1 before winning the seventh game too.

Game 7, Wednesday, October 20, was on a chilly but clear night. Ace vs. ace: Andujar, back after his injury last Friday, against Vuckovich.

Early indications were that Andujar was on, Vuckovich off. With an aching knee but determined not to let anything beat him, the Cardinals' right-hander threw three perfect innings, then stranded a single runner in the fourth. The Cardinals put baserunners everywhere but failed to score in the first few innings.

However, in their fourth, they tallied in typical fashion: singles by McGee and Herr that put runners at the corners, and an infield single by Lonnie Smith brought McGee home.

Up to that point, the Cardinals had tied the Brewers in homers, 4–4. As if to reclaim their image, the Brewers tied the game in their fifth when Oglivie led off by hitting one deep over the right-field wall.

Then the Brewers seemed to take charge of things when they plated a pair in the sixth. Gantner led off with a double and scored when Andujar threw Molitor's bunt into right field. Molitor moved to third on the next play then scored on a sacrifice fly by Cooper.

But in this back-and-forth game, the Cardinals quickly rebounded in their half of inning six. With one out Ozzie Smith singled and went to third on Lonnie Smith's double. Kuenn, who stuck with his starters, pulled Vuckovich for Bob McClure; Gene Tenace again batted for Oberkfell. The former Oakland A's catcher had been unsuccessful several times in that role but this time walked, to be replaced on the bases by a leaner Mike Ramsey.

Keith Hernandez then celebrated his twenty-ninth birthday by driving home the Smiths with a sharp single that also sent Ramsey to third. Hendrick then slapped a pitch on the outside part of the plate to right field, and the Cardinals had the lead.

Andujar completed his work in the seventh, but not without a moment of controversy fueled by Milwaukee's brewing frustration. With two out and a man on first, second baseman Jim Gantner rapped one back at Andujar, who stabbed it then, in his trademarked manner, fired the ball to first for the final out. Also part of Andujar's manner was his hollering at an opposing batter who'd hit one back at him.

He did. Gantner responded. The umps moved in, but it was the typical baseball altercation: no hits.

Sutter then did what they paid him top dollar—reportedly $950,000 in 1982—to do. He retired the last six batters. For good measure, the Cardinals scored two more in their eighth. When Steve Braun lined a single to center for the final run, center fielder Gorman Thomas' face and mannerisms clearly showed his dejection as he looked down and held the ball momentarily before returning it to the infield.

Thomas would be the last out in the ninth, but not before fouling off—some sharply, some weakly—four split-fingered fastballs on a three-two count. The on-its-feet crowd had to reset its emotions after every pitch. Sutter had made his living by that pitch, which appeared to drop almost straight down as it neared the plate. He'd learned it in the mid-1970s as a struggling minor-league starter. It had propelled him to a Cy Young Award in 1979, perennial leadership in NL saves, and the recognition among many as the best reliever in baseball. After the fourth foul tap he threw a straight fastball. Thinking it would drop, Thomas waved his bat through the air beneath it as it crossed the plate.

Cardinals broadcaster Jack Buck then proclaimed over the airwaves: "A swing and a miss, and that a winner! That's a winner! A World Series winner for the Cardinals!"

Porter, sounding like a happy kid, told TV cameras: "This is the most fun I've had playing baseball in my whole career. I can't believe this." His manager shared his catcher's joy. "That's another reason I'm happy about us winning this. Darrell was with me in those three playoff losses in Kansas City."

While Gussie Busch—decked out in his red vest and red cowboy hat—thanked and embraced Herzog, the fans who'd scaled the outfield walls tore up the synthetic turf, which was faded and in need of replacement anyway. A cop who'd felt bad that he hadn't been able to stop the vandalism tried to apologize to Busch later, only to be told that the news wasn't diminishing the Big Eagle's joy. The next day Busch and his players heard the cheers of tens of thousands along a Downtown parade route.

The Cardinals traded Hernandez in June 1983 not revealing at the time their concern over alleged drug problems. They contended until Labor Day before folding in September. Whitey would rebuild and put NL champs on the field in 1985 and 1987, though both teams were hobbled by injuries and lost the Series. The Brewers, hailed back in Milwaukee despite their Series loss, faltered in 1983, and Kuenn was fired at the end of the season. A gamer who'd battled health problems, he died of a heart attack in 1988.

1982 Line Scores

Game 1, Tuesday, October 12, at Busch Stadium, St. Louis

	1 2 3 4 5 6 7 8 9	R	H	E
Milwaukee	2 0 0 1 1 2 0 0 4	10	17	0
St. Louis	0 0 0 0 0 0 0 0 0	0	3	1

W—Caldwell L—Forsch
Time—2:30 Attendance—53,723

Summary: Brewers' hit machine took page from Cardinals book and wore down Redbirds with thirteen singles and Ted Simmons' homer. Cards castoff Mike Caldwell scattered three hits in route-going whitewash.

Game 2, Wednesday, October 13, at Busch Stadium

	1 2 3 4 5 6 7 8 9	R	H	E
Milwaukee	0 1 2 0 1 0 0 0 0	4	10	1
St. Louis	0 0 2 0 0 2 0 1 x	5	8	0

W—Sutter L—McClure
Time—2:54 Attendance—53,723

Summary: Darrell Porter silenced critics with two-run double tying the game, then Cards used bases-loaded walk to take lead while Bruce Sutter shut down Brewers over last 2 1/3 innings.

Game 3, Friday, October 15, at County Stadium, Milwaukee

	1 2 3 4 5 6 7 8 9	R	H	E
St. Louis	0 0 0 0 3 0 2 0 1	6	6	1
Milwaukee	0 0 0 0 0 0 0 2 0	2	5	3

W—Andujar L—Vuckovich
Time—2:53 Attendance—56,556

Summary: Rookie Willie McGee had one of best Series games in history, poling two home runs for Cardinals and preventing one by Brewers with ninth-inning catch.

Game 4, Saturday, October 16, at County Stadium

	1 2 3 4 5 6 7 8 9	R	H	E
St. Louis	1 3 0 0 0 1 0 0 0	5	8	1
Milwaukee	0 0 0 0 1 0 6 0 x	7	10	2

W—Slaton L—Bair S—McClure
Time—3:04 Attendance—56,560

Summary: Costly error by pitcher Dave LaPoint while covering first opened flood gates for Brewers in seventh inning and wiped out Cardinals lead, tying Series at two each.

Game 5, Sunday, October 17, at County Stadium

	1 2 3 4 5 6 7 8 9	R	H	E
St. Louis	0 0 1 0 0 0 1 0 2	4	15	2
Milwaukee	1 0 1 0 1 0 1 2 x	6	11	1

W—Caldwell L—Forsch S—McClure
Time—3:02 Attendance—56,562

Summary: Mike Caldwell gave up 14 hits, but Milwaukee offense made Cardinals play catch-up all day. Brewers roughed up Bruce Sutter in eighth, and Cardinals rally in last frame fell short.

Game 6, Tuesday, October 19, at Busch Stadium

	1 2 3 4 5 6 7 8 9	R	H	E
Milwaukee	0 0 0 0 0 0 0 0 1	1	4	4
St. Louis	0 2 0 3 2 6 0 0 x	13	12	1

W—Stuper L—Sutton
Time—2:21 Attendance—53,723

Summary: Rookie John Stuper came within two outs of a lopsided shutout in a game delayed twice by rain. Dane Iorg's three extra-base hits led the Cards' attack.

Game 7, Wednesday, October 20, at Busch Stadium

	1 2 3 4 5 6 7 8 9	R	H	E
Milwaukee	0 0 0 0 1 2 0 0 0	3	7	0
St. Louis	0 0 0 1 0 3 0 2 x	6	15	1

W—Andujar L—McClure S—Sutter
Time—2:50 Attendance—53,723

Summary: Cardinals claimed ninth world title with comeback win, sparked by Andujar's pitching, Hernandez and Hendrick's hitting, and Sutter's closing.

Total attendance: 384,570
Total gate receipts: $6,421,055.31
Cardinals player's share: $43,279.69

17

2006

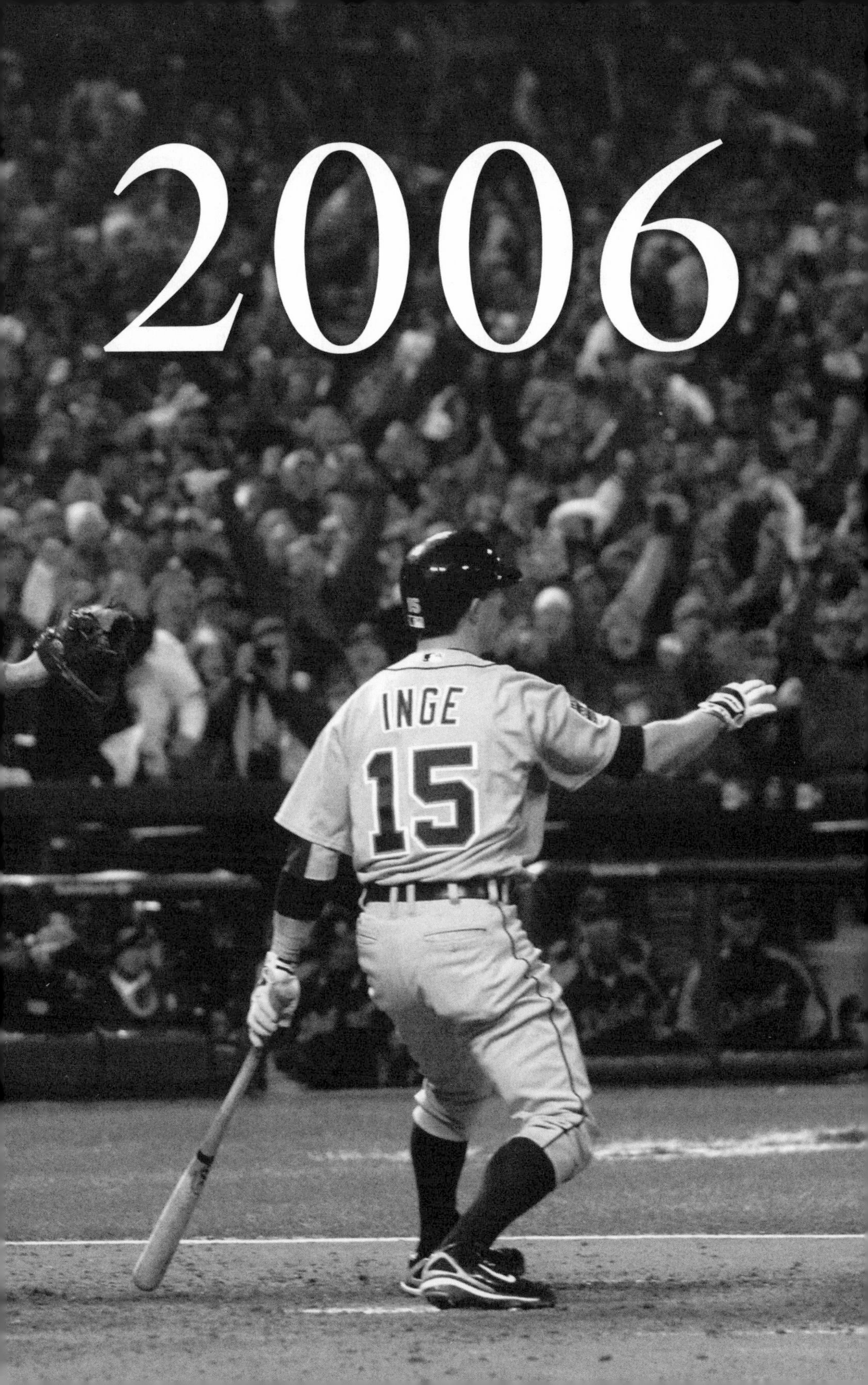

Cardinals Defeat Tigers 4 Games to 1

GAME 1:	CARDINALS	7	TIGERS	2
GAME 2:	CARDINALS	1	TIGERS	3
GAME 3:	CARDINALS	5	TIGERS	0
GAME 4:	CARDINALS	5	TIGERS	4
GAME 5:	CARDINALS	4	TIGERS	2

REGULAR-SEASON STARTING LINEUP		
David Eckstein	ss	.292
Chris Duncan	lf	22 HRs in 280 at-bats
Albert Pujols	1b	.331, 49 HRs, 137 RBIs
Scott Rolen	3b	.296, 22 HRs, 95 RBIs
Juan Encarnacion	rf	.278
Jim Edmonds	cf	19 HRs, 70 RBIs
Yadier Molina	c	led NL catchers with 79 assists
Aaron Miles	2b	.263

PITCHERS		
Chris Carpenter	15-8	222 innings
Jeff Suppan	12-7	2.39 ERA after All-Star break
Jason Marquis	14-16	6.02 ERA
Jeff Weaver	5-4	acquired in July
Anthony Reyes	5-8	5.06 ERA
Adam Wainwright	2-1	3.12 ERA in 61 games
Jason Isringhausen	4-8	33 saves, 10 blown saves

BENCH	
Ronnie Belliard	inf
Scott Spiezio	inf
So Taguchi	of
Preston Wilson	of

How the Cardinals Got to the World Series:

The Cardinals led the National League Central Division from June 9 through the end of the season but nearly lost a seven-game lead in the final two weeks and finished with an 83–78 final record, just 1½ games ahead of Houston. In the first playoff round they upset San Diego (88–74 in the regular season) three games to one, and in the NL Championship Series they beat the heavily favored New York Mets (97–65) four games to three.

The Cardinals' Series Opponent:

Under new manager Jim Leyland, the Detroit Tigers improved from 71–91 in 2005 to 95–67 in 2006. As the AL wild card team, the Tigers lost the first game of the playoffs and then proceeded to win seven in a row to eliminate first the Yankees and then the Athletics. The Tigers had four hitters with twenty-five or more home runs: Craig Monroe, Brandon Inge, Marcus Thames, and Magglio Ordonez, while their leader in batting average (.320) and runs scored (104) was shortstop Carlos Guillen. The real strength of the team was pitching, with fastballers Justin Verlander and Jeremy Bonderman and soft-tossers Nate Robertson and Kenny Rogers leading the starting staff. Flamethrowers Joel Zumaya and Fernando Rodney set up veteran Todd Jones in the bullpen.

Game Balls and Gamers

The Cardinals had just won the first playoff game of the 2006 postseason, beating the Padres in San Diego. It was one more victory than some cynics thought they would get, and one more game than the critics thought they deserved to play. But they had played and won. Now the oldest veteran on the roster, Jim Edmonds, stood on a couch in the visitors' clubhouse, called his teammates together for an impromptu ceremony, and presented a game ball to one of the team's newest additions, Ronnie Belliard, for his outstanding defensive play in the game. A new ritual was born that would help carry the Cardinals to their unlikeliest World Championship.

After having won one hundred or more games in both 2004 and 2005, the 2006 Cardinals were expected to dominate again. The first ten weeks of the season went more or less according to plan, and through June 18 the team was 42–26 with a 5½ game lead. But then the Birds began spinning their wheels. Starter Mark Mulder went down with shoulder trouble in June, and shortstop David Eckstein missed a month starting in mid-August with a strained oblique muscle. Center fielder Jim Edmonds missed most of September with dizziness following a collision with the fence. Closer Jason Isringhausen's bad hip sapped his effectiveness, and he called it quits for the season in early September.

Luckily, no NL Central Division rival was able to mount much of a challenge. Although Cincinnati shaved the St. Louis lead to percentage points on a couple of occasions, the Cardinals had a comfortable seven-game lead with just thirteen games left to play. Then suddenly the Astros launched a nine-game winning streak while the Redbirds lost seven straight. With four games left, the lead had been reduced to just a half game. Cardinals wins on the final Friday and Saturday averted disaster, and on the final scheduled day, they needed only a win or a Houston loss to clinch the division pennant. A St. Louis loss and a Houston win would force the Cardinals to make up a rainout on Monday, and if they lost that one, there would be a tie-breaker in Houston on Tuesday.

With staff ace Chris Carpenter well rested, Manager Tony La Russa opted to start rookie Anthony Reyes on Sunday and save Carp for Monday. The gamble looked bad early on, as Reyes was knocked out in the very first inning and the Cards lost 5–3. Luckily, Houston lost in Atlanta, and the Cardinals clinched the division title anyway.

Having barely averted a collapse for the ages, St. Louis was matched up against San Diego in the first round of the playoffs. The Padres had battled the Dodgers to a tie in the NL West and had earned the division crown because of the tie-breaker. They had the best team ERA in the league and were especially strong in the bullpen, with all-time saves leader Trevor Hoffman adding a league-best forty-six in 2006. San Diego had beaten the Cardinals in four out of six regular-season matchups.

The Padres were favored to win the series, but the Cardinals, "having avoided a nightmare finish," as La Russa put it, were rejuvenated. Suddenly their whole projected starting lineup was healthy enough to play, although Scott Rolen's weak shoulder limited his production, and Jim Edmonds was hobbling on a sore foot that required daily pain-killing and Lydocaine injections. "The shots aren't fun, but it's definitely worth it," Jimmy Ballgame said. "I love being in the playoffs."

Tony's Sunday gamble meant that Carpenter could pitch in Game 1 on Tuesday, October 3. Then the breaks started to go St. Louis's way. With a man on base and the game tied 0–0 in the top of the fourth, Albert Pujols lifted a pop foul behind home plate. Catcher Mike Piazza went back to the screen but stumbled as he was trying to glove the ball, and it fell safely. After a couple of two-strike fouls, Pujols launched a mammoth home run over the Padre bullpen, giving the Cardinals a 2–0 lead. San Diego starter Jake Peavy was knocked out in the sixth inning as St. Louis built a 5–0 lead.

The Padres got a run in the sixth and then made their bid in the seventh inning after Russell Branyan's one-out triple got past Jim Edmonds's dive. After a walk, La Russa took Carpenter out of the game. Left-handed rookie Tyler Johnson came in, and his first pitch was wild. But it somehow hit the batter on the foot, preventing Branyan from scoring. With the bases now loaded, Johnson fanned Mark Bellhorn. Todd Walker cracked a grass-clipper toward right field, apparently ticketed for a two-run single, but second baseman Ronnie Belliard dove to his left, tackled the ball, managed to corral it while rolling over, and threw the batter out at first. That saved the game and the Cardinals won by a tidy 5–1 final score.

After the game, Edmonds presented Belliard with a game ball. The veteran said he "just wanted to do something for the boys." After all, La Russa had told him, "If you have something to say, say it," Edmonds recalled later. His manager also reflected that "I believe that Jim realized that, 'Whoa, this could be my last and best chance.'" So he "did what he did, which was be very vocal and give us a real spiritual lift."

For Game 2 on Thursday, La Russa tapped Jeff Weaver to start. Weaver had been let go by the Angels in July after compiling a 3–10 record with an embarrassing 6.29 ERA. With the Redbirds he had gone 5–4, though his ERA was still an ugly 5.14. He had had extra trouble pitching at home, so he got the Game 2 start at

San Diego. Relying mostly on curveballs, Weaver held the opposition to no runs and two hits in five innings of work. Four relief pitchers, Randy Flores, Josh Kinney, Johnson, and Adam Wainwright, closed out the shutout with four combined scoreless innings. Pujols singled home the first Cardinals run in the fourth inning and scored after an adventuresome gambol around the bases. Edmonds gamely legged out an infield hit for the RBI, but it took him another fifteen or twenty yards past first base to finally limp to a stop. Those were the only runs in a 2–0 game.

Towering Curt Young spoiled the clinching party back in St. Louis by beating the Birds and Jeff Suppan on Saturday, 3–1. But the Cardinals got the job done against old teammate Woody Williams in Game 4 on Sunday, 6–2. Carpenter pitched the clincher, and Juan Encarnacion earned a game ball with the game-winning RBI triple in the victors' four-run, sixth-inning rally. A rare bases-loaded squeeze bunt by David Eckstein capped that rally, and St. Louis was back in the National League Championship Series for the third consecutive season.

The NLCS versus the heavily favored Mets opened a day late due to rain on Thursday, October 12, at Shea Stadium. For the first game and most of the second contest, the series went as expected, with the Mets dominating. Veteran Tom Glavine and two relievers shut St. Louis out in the opener, 2–0, with Cardinal-killer Carlos Beltran socking a two-run home run off of Weaver. In Game 2, Carlos Delgado blasted two opposite-field homers against Carpenter, and the Mets led 6–4 through six innings. But with two out in the seventh, Pujols singled, Edmonds walked, and Scott Spiezio hooked a deep one into the right-field corner for a game-tying triple. The tie held until the ninth, when little-used So Taguchi battled relief ace Billy Wagner for eight pitches before finally lining a home run onto the bullpen cover in left field. Piling on, Pujols and Spiezio both doubled and scored, and the Cardinals had a come-from-behind 9–6 win to even the series.

Spiezio had started at third base in place of Rolen, who had gone one for eleven in the San Diego series before finally admitting that his shoulder needed medical attention. After a month of prevarications, he now had taken his medicine: a cortisone shot and anti-inflammatory medication. But he had been hitless in the first game against the Mets and was left out of the lineup, and Rolen was vocal in his displeasure. La Russa offered no apologies, "I'm just trying to win the game, buddy," was his reply.

The guy who won Game 3 was Jeff Suppan, who pitched eight shutout innings for the Cardinals and hit a rare home run of his own. Though Rolen started at third (and would start every subsequent postseason game), Spiezio, starting in left field, once again delivered a big blow, a two-run pop-fly triple that landed just fair down the right-field line. The St. Louis crowd reveled in the 5–0 victory.

New York bounced right back, winning a 12–5 slugfest in Game 4. Yadier Molina, Jim Edmonds, and little David Eckstein homered for St. Louis, but Carlos Beltran hit two solo homers and scored four runs for New York, David Wright hit a two-run four-bagger, and Carlos Delgado had a three-run homer and a two-run double to pace the Mets rout.

Rain providentially postponed Game 5 from Monday to Tuesday night, allowing both scheduled starting pitchers to have their normal rest. This time Weaver got the better of Glavine, winning 4–2. Pujols, limping on a sore hamstring, lined a homer for the Cards' first run (and Albert's only RBI of the series) in the fourth inning, and Preston Wilson's double up the right-center-field gap in the fifth put St. Louis ahead to stay. When La Russa sent left-handed Chris Duncan to pinch-hit for Weaver in the sixth against southpaw Pedro Feliciano, some questioned his strategy. But not after Duncan unloaded with a home run. Deft use of the bullpen and hitter matchups nailed down the 4–2 Cardinals win.

Needing to win one out of two in New York to pull off the upset and advance to the World Series, the Cardinals came up empty in Game 6. Carpenter allowed a leadoff home run to Jose Reyes in the first inning, and the Mets never trailed. Taguchi's two-out, two-run double off of Wagner in the ninth prevented a shutout, but St. Louis lost soundly, 4–2.

So it all came down to Game 7. Workmanlike Jeff Suppan would pitch for the Cardinals, unheralded Oliver Perez for the Mets. New York scratched a run in the bottom of the first, and St. Louis answered in the top of the second when a neat push bunt by Belliard plated Edmonds. As the score stayed at 1–1, the tension mounted, especially in the action-packed sixth inning. For St. Louis, Edmonds walked with one out, and Rolen followed with a long drive over the bullpen fence in left. Unfortunately for the Cardinals, outfielder Endy Chavez made a racing, leaping, miraculous snow-cone catch, bringing the ball back into play and doubling Edmonds off first for good measure. In the New York half, Delgado walked with one gone, and Wright grounded one toward the hole in the left side. Rolen was able to glove the ball, but his throw to first sailed majestically into the seats, putting runners on second and third. Suppan remained calm in the crisis, however, getting Valentin to fan on a changeup and then retiring Chavez on a routine fly ball.

Both starting pitchers were gone by the ninth inning. Mets reliever Aaron Heilman retired the first hitter and then got ahead of Rolen, 0–2. But the veteran gamer battled back and singled on the ninth pitch of the at-bat. Molina only saw one pitch, a hanging changeup, and he launched it into the left-field bullpen for a two-run home run, silencing the Shea faithful. Wainwright was brought in to pitch the bottom of the ninth and was in hot water immediately. Valentin served a soft single over second, and Chavez lined a clean hit to left. A called third strike and a fly out put the Birds one out away, but Paul LoDuca walked on five pitches, loading the bases. The hitter was Beltran, who had raked Cardinals pitching for four homers in the 2004 NLCS and three more in this series. Wainwright's first fastball was a called strike. The second one was fouled off. Then came a curveball. Beltran was frozen by the change in speed, and the pitch broke over the heart of the plate for a called strike three, perhaps the most memorable strike in Cardinals history. As the stunned New York crowd watched in silence, the Cardinals mobbed Wainwright and Molina on the mound. Champagne was splashed in the clubhouse, and post-game interviews were delayed while game balls were presented to Molina and Suppan. The Cardinals were headed for their seventeenth World Series. The champagne still flowed on the Cardinals flight to Detroit for the opening of the World Series, and the Redbirds were feeling on top of the world. "I smiled myself to sleep," Wainwright quipped.

Las Vegas sports books listed the Tigers as 2–1 favorites to win the championship. With the hiring of veteran manager Jim Leyland, the Tigers had made a miraculous turnaround in 2006, winning ninety-five regular-season games following just seventy-one wins in 2005. Detroit had sported the best record in baseball for most of the summer and had swept a three-game interleague series against St. Louis. But the Tigers had stumbled down the stretch, losing thirty-one of their final fifty games, and settled for the Wild Card berth in the playoffs. After losing their first postseason game, they ran off seven consecutive victories, ousting the mighty Yankees in the first round and sweeping the A's in the ALCS. That gave them six days off before the start of the World Series. Leyland was a close friend Cardinals skipper La Russa, and the two kept in constant touch through the season. But the friendship and the contact would be suspended for the World Series.

La Russa and pitching coach Dave Duncan had developed a reputation over the years for preferring veteran players, especially pitchers, over youngsters. But in 2006 they had used young guns like Johnson, Flores, Kinney, and Wainwright in numerous critical situations with good results. For Saturday's Game 1 of the World Series, they would start a twenty-five-year-old rookie, Anthony Reyes, against Tiger rookie Justin Verlander. Reyes weathered a rough first inning, limiting the damage to one run, and then pitched beautifully. Using mainly inside fastballs, he handcuffed the Detroit batters, retiring seventeen in a row at one point. He did not falter until yielding a leadoff home run in the ninth inning.

After a quick top of the first, Detroit got one run and had men on second and third before Reyes finally got the third out. But the game turned quickly in St. Louis's favor. Scott Rolen, who had been hitless in the 2004 Fall Classic, homered in his first 2006 World Series at-bat in the second inning to tie the score. With two out in the Cardinals third, Chris Duncan's RBI double gave the Birds the lead. Albert Pujols, who had had no RBIs in the 2004 Series, then lined a two-run drive over the right-field wall to make it 4–1 in favor of St. Louis. A wild pickoff throw by Verlander and a double error by third baseman Brandon Inge (complete with an obstruction ruling) handed St. Louis three more runs in the sixth. The Cards won by a 7–2 score.

In Sunday's Game 2, it was forty-one-year-old Kenny Rogers's turn in the spotlight. The veteran Detroit lefty seemed to have something on his left palm in the first inning, dirt or pine tar, perhaps, and the Cardinals complained to the umpires. The stain was gone in the second inning, and Rogers dominated, with or without foreign substances, into the eighth inning, allowing only two hits, three walks, and a hit batsman. Jeff Weaver, starting for the Cardinals, pitched credibly, but Craig Monroe's home run in the first and Carlos Guillen's double in the first and triple in the fifth earned Detroit three runs. An error by Detroit closer Todd Jones allowed St. Louis to tally in the ninth, but the Tigers had an easy 3–1 win to even the Series.

In Game 3 in St. Louis, Cardinals ace Chris Carpenter outdid Reyes and Rogers, pitching eight full innings of three-hit, no-walk baseball, allowing only one runner to get past first base. His impassive demeanor and aggressive approach evoked memories of Bob

Gibson, as he used inside fastballs and pinpoint sinkers and cutters to break several Tigers bats. Nate Robertson took the loss for Detroit, although he allowed only two fourth-inning runs. Preston Wilson opened the rally with a hit to left center. Robertson tried to keep the ball away from Pujols, but Albert stepped into a 3–1 pitch and served one down the right-field line for a ground-rule double. After a walk and a force out at home, Jim Edmonds uppercut a topspinner past the first baseman for a two-run double.

Reliever Joel Zumaya made a disastrous, two-run throwing error on a potential double-play ball in the sixth, and Zach Miner unfurled a run-scoring wild pitch in the seventh to pad the St. Louis lead. Looper pitched a scoreless ninth for St. Louis to close out the 5–0 verdict. A cold rain postponed Wednesday's scheduled Game 4, and the field was still soggy on Thursday. The Tigers started out as if they meant to turn the Series around, with Sean Casey raking Suppan for a homer in the second and an RBI single in the third as Detroit took an early 3–0 lead. The Cardinals got one run in their half of the third when Aaron Miles opened with a liner that fell just in front of Curtis Granderson's dive in center field. After stealing second, Miles coasted home on David Eckstein's line-drive double over the shortstop. The Cardinals cut the deficit to 3–2 in the fourth when Rolen and Molina both doubled down the left-field line.

The Tigers coughed up the lead in the seventh inning. Eckstein opened with a routine fly to center, but Granderson lost his footing, somersaulted, and was too late getting back up to catch the ball, which went for a gift double. Taguchi laid down a sacrifice bunt, and pitcher Fernando Rodney obliged with the Tigers' daily error, throwing it far over first base, allowing Eckstein to score the tying run and Taguchi to advance to second base with no one out. After an intentional pass to Pujols, Rodney fanned both Edmonds and Rolen. But Wilson's sharp grounder found a hole, and Taguchi raced home with the go-ahead run.

Detroit was not quite ready to call it quits, however, tying the game in the top of the eighth on doubles by Ivan Rodriguez and Brandon Inge. But in the bottom half, they gave the run right back. New pitcher Joel Zumaya walked Yadier Molina on four pitches to start the inning, though Miles then hit into a force out. Juan Encarnacion, benched because of a sore wrist, struck out as a pinch-hitter, but the last strike was a wild pitch, sending Miles to second. Eckstein lifted a two-out drive toward left center, where left fielder Monroe had a little trouble getting traction and eventually made a diving try. The ball ticked off the tip of his glove, however, for another tainted double for Eckstein, this one driving home the go-ahead run. Wainwright worked a one-two-three ninth, and the Cardinals had a 5–4 victory, leaving them one win away from the World Championship.

That championship was won at home on Friday, October 27. Because of the Wednesday rainout, La Russa was able to jump Weaver ahead of Reyes to pitch Game 5. Verlander got the start for Leyland. Verlander looked shaky in the first inning, throwing two wild pitches, but he escaped a bases-loaded jam unscathed. But another Tigers mistake helped the Cards score one in the second. With two out and Molina on third, Eckstein hit a broken-bat grounder over the third-base bag, where Inge made a diving stop. But his hurried throw to first was wild, and the hitter motored around to second as the runner trotted home.

A Cardinals misplay was costly in the fourth. Magglio Ordonez hit an easy fly to right field, where Chris Duncan made a clean muff. Sean Casey followed with a home run near the foul line, and the Tigers suddenly had a 2–1 lead.

But they gave the lead right back in the bottom of the fourth. With one out Molina and Taguchi singled. Pitcher Weaver bunted hard enough to give the Tigers a chance to get the lead runner. But Verlander, unbelievably yet somehow inevitably, threw the ball away down the left-field line, allowing Molina to come around to score while Taguchi and Weaver wound up on second and third. Leyland was so rattled by yet another error by his pitchers that he kept the infield back, and Eckstein's routine grounder to short sent home the go-ahead run—the World Series–winning run as it turned out.

St. Louis added an insurance run in the seventh when Eckstein beat out a bouncer to short, Guillen inexplicably laying back on the ball. Rolen's two-out single brought Eckstein home. The two St. Louis left-side infielders, Rolen and Eckstein, tied for the team lead in hits in the Series with eight each, and Eck got the nod as World Series MVP. With Weaver pitching his best game in a St. Louis uniform, the Tigers mounted no serious threats through the eighth inning. Wainwright closed out the ninth with a zero, despite a walk and a hit, fanning Inge to end the game and start the celebration.

So the Cardinals were World Champions for the tenth time. For this one they had pulled off upsets in three rounds of postseason play, each time beating a team that had bested them in regular-season competition. The unexpected nature of the triumph made it all the sweeter to the players and coaches. La Russa and Rolen even hugged in the post-game euphoria.

After five games played in frigid conditions, Sunday dawned sunny and warm as half a million fans swarmed downtown St. Louis for the Cardinals victory parade. As ecstatic as the onlookers were, the players may have been even giddier. "I never thought I'd have this feeling. And I can't describe it," Carpenter declared. "I've been dreaming of this all my life," Pujols crowed. But it's doubtful anyone was more moved by the championship than La Russa. "When you're around here you can't join the club unless you win the World Series," he had reflected on Friday. After toiling here for ten seasons without a World Series title, Tony had finally joined the club. At long last "our World Championship dream came true," he told Cardinal Nation. "Let's enjoy it."

The brilliant playoff run in 2006 had precious little carryover into 2007. Chris Carpenter pitched only on Opening Day and missed the rest of the season. Albert Pujols was gimpy on the bases most of the year. Scott Rolen finally submitted to shoulder surgery again in September. And the team finished under .500 for the first time in the new century.

2006 Line Scores

Game 1, Saturday, October 21, at Comerica Park, Detroit

	1	2	3	4	5	6	7	8	9	R	H	E
St. Louis	0	1	3	0	0	3	0	0	0	7	8	2
Detroit	1	0	0	0	0	0	0	0	1	2	4	3

W—Reyes L—Verlander

Time—2:54 Attendance—42,479

Summary: Anthony Reyes pitched into the ninth inning, stifling the Tiger bats. Scott Rolen's home run got the Cardinals on the board, Chris Duncan's double put them ahead, and Albert Pujols's two-run homer on the very next pitch gave them some breathing room.

Game 2, Sunday, October 22, at Comerica Park

	1	2	3	4	5	6	7	8	9	R	H	E
St. Louis	0	0	0	0	0	0	0	0	1	1	4	1
Detroit	2	0	0	0	1	0	0	0	x	3	10	1

W—Rogers L—Weaver S—Jones

Time—2:55 Attendance—42,533

Summary: Kenny Rogers blanked the Birds for eight innings, allowing only two hits. Craig Monroe's home run scored the Tigers' first run, and Carlos Guillen added an RBI double in the first and a triple and run scored in the fifth.

Game 3, Tuesday, October 24, at Busch Stadium, St. Louis

	1	2	3	4	5	6	7	8	9	R	H	E
Detroit	0	0	0	0	0	0	0	0	0	0	3	1
St. Louis	0	0	0	2	0	0	2	1	x	5	7	0

W—Carpenter L—Robertson

Time—3:03 Attendance—46,513

Summary: Chris Carpenter pitched eight innings, allowing just three hits, and Braden Looper finished the shutout. Jim Edmonds's two-run double put St. Louis ahead, and a two-run throwing error and a run-scoring wild pitch made it a 5–0 final.

Game 4, Thursday, October 26, at Busch Stadium

	1	2	3	4	5	6	7	8	9	R	H	E
Detroit	0	1	2	0	0	0	0	1	0	4	10	1
St. Louis	0	0	1	1	0	0	2	1	x	5	9	0

W—Wainwright L—Zumaya
Time—3:35 Attendance—46,470

Summary: After falling behind early, the Cardinals took the lead in the seventh thanks to a gift double and a throwing error by the pitcher. Brandon Inge's RBI double in the top of the eighth knotted the count, but David Eckstein's fourth hit of the game, a double just off the outfielder's glove, plated the winning run in the bottom of the round.

Game 5, Friday, October 27, at Busch Stadium

	1	2	3	4	5	6	7	8	9	R	H	E
Detroit	0	0	0	2	0	0	0	0	0	2	5	2
St. Louis	0	1	0	2	0	0	1	0	x	4	8	1

W—Weaver L—Verlander S—Wainwright
Time—2:56 Attendance—46,638

Summary: Weaver pitched eight innings, allowing only one earned run. The first two Cardinal runs came home on throwing errors, and Eckstein's infield out allowed So Taguchi to score the go-ahead tally in the fourth inning. Adam Wainwright pitched around a hit and a walk in the ninth to wrap up the Cardinals' tenth World Championship.

Total attendance: 224,633
Cardinals player's share: $362,173

Appendixes

"Winner Takes All"—St. Louis's First World Series Champion

The concept of a baseball World Series dates back to the 1880s, when the champions of the two rival major leagues of the time, the National League and the American Association, arranged to play each other after the pennant races were over. Initially billed as being "for the championship of the United States," these postseason matchups were called the "World Series" by the end of the decade.

The St. Louis Browns, winners of four consecutive American Association pennants from 1885 through 1888, participated in a postseason series each year. In 1885 they arranged a traveling series of up to twelve games in seven cities against the National League champion Chicago White Stockings (later renamed the Cubs).

After one game in Chicago and three in St. Louis (one of which ended in a rancorous forfeit win for Chicago), the teams traveled to Pittsburgh and Cincinnati in hopes of going farther east. But because of disappointing crowds in those neutral sites, the teams agreed to make the seventh scheduled game, in Cincinnati, the final. Chicago's captain, Adrian Anson, first said his team would forget about the forfeit win, reverting to a 2–2 tie in games to be settled by that Cincinnati match. But after the Browns won, claiming the world title three games to two, Chicago president Albert

Spalding took back the forfeit win and declared the series a draw, which history books to this day proclaim, though 1885 newspapers said the Browns were world champs.

Both teams repeated as pennant winners in 1886 and arranged a rematch. This time, however, it was determined to play only a best-of-seven series with three games in each home city, and a seventh game, if necessary, at a neutral site. Given the bad blood engendered by the year before's fiasco, the two owners agreed that the winning team would get all the gate receipts. The White Stockings took two of the first three games, all in Chicago, but the Browns won all three games in St. Louis to claim the championship.

The Browns' 4–3 win in the finale featured a dramatic comeback and then an extra-inning run scored by center fielder Curt Welch on a wild pitch. Browns owner Chris Von der Ahe gave the players half of the total winnings of $13,920, a winners' share of around $580—more than most of their working-class fans earned in a full year.

The Browns won two more pennants, in 1887 and 1888, but lost extended Series to National League champion Detroit in 1887 (ten games to five) and New York in 1888 (six games to four). In 1892, the St. Louis Browns were among the American Association teams taken into the NL when the rival leagues were merged. The nickname "Browns" was changed to "Cardinals" in 1900. The modern World Series between the NL and AL began in 1903.

A Note on the Ballparks and Leagues the Cardinals Played In

Ballparks

The Cardinals have hosted World Series games in three different baseball parks, two of which no longer exist.

From 1920 through 1952 they played in Sportsman's Park, at Grand Boulevard and Dodier Avenue in North St. Louis, today the site of the Herbert Hoover Boys Club. Originally a wooden structure from the 1870s, the park had been renovated and expanded in steel and concrete several times in the 1900s. It conformed to the rectangular shape of the city block it completely covered. Automobile parking was minimal, which was not a problem in the years before the end of World War II, when many people rode plentiful buses and streetcars to games.

Sportsman's Park seated, at most, in the lower 30,000 range. It had a double-decked grandstand covering the foul territory area between the foul poles, uncovered bleachers in left field with a large scoreboard behind it along Sullivan Avenue, and a covered pavilion in right field running along Grand Boulevard. The distance from home plate to the left-field line was 354 feet for most of its years and 426 feet to deepest center. The right-field line was only 310 feet, but in most years Sportsman's Park had a 30-foot-high screen above the 11-foot wall from the foul line to the 354-foot sign in right center. In the early years the flagpole was in center field in front of the wall, another hazard for outfielders to contend with.

In 1953 the Anheuser-Busch brewery bought the Cardinals from Fred Saigh and Sportsman's Park from the St. Louis Browns, who moved to Baltimore the following year. New owner Gussie Busch improved the ballpark's look and comfort for the fans and renamed it Busch Stadium. But he left the park's playing dimensions and field layout the same. The Cardinals played there—including the 1964 World Series—until moving to the new Civic Center Busch Memorial Stadium in May 1966.

The multi-purpose Busch Memorial Stadium was built after the razing of old warehouses as part of a massive downtown redevelopment that included putting a Gateway Arch on the riverfront. While the Bi-State transit system ran Redbird Express buses to and from suburban shopping centers to the stadium, most fans drove to the games and found ample parking in new, nearby, multi-storied garages. The stadium was named Busch after the largest single contributor to the $20 million project—Anheuser-Busch.

The 55,000-seat circular stadium, built by private investment, was a big bowl whose surrounding upper-deck design at the apex mimicked the shape of the Arch. It had a symmetrical look and feel, with a small bleacher section in both left and right field's lower deck. The St. Louis Cardinals of the National Football League used it, and the stadium was the site of special events, such as a Beatles concert in 1966. For its first four seasons it had natural grass, giving way in 1970 to AstroTurf. The playing-field dimensions were 330 feet down both foul lines, 386 feet to the power alleys in left and right center, and 414 feet to dead center. The Cardinals played there through 2005. After new ownership, headed by Bill DeWitt, took over in 1996, they lowered the outfield walls, shortening the power alleys and center field by 10 feet. Real grass and a dirt infield replaced the artificial turf.

The current Busch Stadium opened in 2006. A "retro" design

with a 46,000 total capacity, it features a 336-foot left-field line, a 335-foot right-field line, 385 feet to the power alleys, and 400 feet to straightaway center. The new stadium was named Busch after the then-St. Louis–based brewery bought the naming rights through 2025.

Leagues

The Cardinals franchise has played in the National League since 1892. From 1900 through 1961, it was an eight-team league, with every team scheduled to play the other seven teams an equal number of times, half at home, each season, usually for a total of 154 games though in a few years it was 140. The pennant winner was the team with the best won-lost record at the end of the season. There were no divisions or wild card teams.

From 1962 through 1968, the Cardinals played in the ten-team NL. Each team was scheduled to play each of its opponents eighteen times, half at home, for a total of 162 games. There were no divisions or wild cards, and the pennant winner was the club with the best won-lost record.

The year 1969 introduced postseason league playoffs to Major League Baseball. The NL and AL each expanded to twelve teams, divided into six-team Eastern and Western divisions. The Cardinals were in the Eastern Division. Each club was scheduled to play its five divisional rivals eighteen times, half at home, and the six teams in the other division twelve times, six at home, a total of 162 games. The two divisional first-place teams met in a playoff to decide the league champion. From 1969 to 1984 it was a best-of-five league championship series, which expanded to best of seven in 1985.

In 1994, the two-division system was altered. Three divisions were created—Eastern, Central, and Western, with the Cardinals moving to the Central. Through 2011, the total number of scheduled games remains 162, with 81 at home. But no two teams, as of this writing, play the same schedule because of differences in the number of home and road games against each divisional rival and because of games with regional competitors from the opposite league (for example, the Cardinals play the Kansas City Royals every season though most of the Cardinals' rivals in the NL Central do not). Also included since 1994 (used first in 1995 because of the players' strike that cancelled the 1994 World Series), has been the use of a wild card team, the club with the best won-lost record after the three divisional winners. Postseason play includes a best-of-five divisional championship series in the first round among the four league contenders, a best-of-seven league championship series, and then the best-of-seven World Series. As of this writing, MLB was considering adding a second wild-card team for 2012.

Bibliography

The information and quotes in this book come from a variety of sources, among them:

Daily and weekly newspapers:

St. Louis newspapers included the *Post-Dispatch*, *Globe-Democrat*, and *Star-Times*; we also consulted microfilm and digital file copies of the weekly *The Sporting News*, once based in St. Louis. Out-of-town newspapers included the *New York Times*, the *Chicago Tribune*, and *USA Today Sports Weekly*.

Periodicals:

The *Baseball Research Journal* and *The National Pastime*, both published by the Society for American Baseball Research, based in Cleveland, were most helpful, as was *Mound City Memories: Baseball in St. Louis*, the official program of SABR's 2007 annual convention in St. Louis.

Annual reference books:

Baseball guides published by Spalding, Reach, and The Sporting News.

Club media guides published by the St. Louis Cardinals.

Official World Series Records (various editions), published by The Sporting News.

Books:

Bob Broeg. *Redbirds: A Century of Cardinals' Baseball.* St. Louis: River City, 1981.

John P. Carmichael, et al. *My Greatest Day in Baseball.* New York: Bison Books, 1945.

Richard M. Cohen, David S. Neft, and Roland T. Johnson, eds. *The World Series.* New York: Dial Press, 1976.

Arthur Daley. *Times at Bat: A Century of Baseball.* New York: Random House, 1950.

Doug Feldmann. *Dizzy Dean and the Gashouse Gang.* Jefferson, N.C.: McFarland & Company, 2000.

Peter Golenbock. *Dynasty: The New York Yankees, 1949-1964.* Englewood Cliffs, N.J.: Dover Publications, 1975.

Peter Golenbock. *The Spirit of St. Louis.* New York: HarperCollins, 2000.

David Halberstam. *October 1964.* New York: Ballantine, 1995.

John Heidenry. *The Gashouse Gang.* New York: Public Affairs, 2007.

Donald Honig. *Baseball: When the Grass Was Real.* New York: Bookthrift, 1975.

Jim Hunstein. *1,2,6,9 & Rogers.* St. Louis: Power Publishing, 2004.

F.C. Lane. *Batting.* Cleveland: SABR, 2001.

Jane Leavy. *The Last Boy: Mickey Mantle and the End of America's Childhood.* New York: Harper, 2010.

Frederick G. Lieb. *The St. Louis Cardinals: The Story of a Great Baseball Team.* New York: G.P. Putnam's Sons, 1947.

Arthur Mann. *Branch Rickey: American in Action.* Boston: Houghton-Mifflin, 1957.

David S. Neft, ed. *The Sports Encyclopedia: Baseball.* New York: St. Martins, 2005.

Rob Rains. *The St. Louis Cardinals: The 100th Anniversary Season.* New York: St. Martins, 1993.

Rob Rains. *Whitey's Boys: A Celebration of the '82 Cards World Championship.* Chicago: Triumph Books, 2002.

Alan Ross. *Cardinals Glory.* St. Louis: Cumberland House, 2005.

John Snyder. *Cardinal Journal.* Cincinnati: Clerisy Press, 2010.

Burt Solomon. *The Baseball Timeline.* New York: Avon Books, 1997.

J. Roy Stockton. *The Gashouse Gang and a Couple of Other Guys.* New York: A. S. Barnes, 1945.

Robert L. Tiemann. *Through the Years at Sportsman's Park.* St. Louis, 1993.

Carson Van Lindt. *One Championship Season: Story of the 1944 St. Louis Browns.* New York: Marabou, 1994.

Fay Vincent. *The Only Game in Town: Baseball Stars of the 1930s and 1940s Talk About the Game They Loved.* New York: Simon & Schuster, 2005.

Websites:

www.baseball-reference.com

www.baseball-almanac.com

www.retrosheet.org

www.heritageresearch.com

Interviews with Chris Carpenter, Marty Marion, Dal Maxvill, Tim McCarver, Red Schoendienst, and John Stuper.

About the Authors

James Rygelski was a newspaper reporter and editor for more than thirty years. He also has contributed articles on baseball history to a variety of publications, including those of the Society for American Baseball Research (SABR). He was co-author, with George Castle, of *The I-55 Series: Cubs vs. Cardinals.* A St. Louis City resident, he works for the St. Louis Public Library.

A lifelong Cardinals fan despite spending much of his youth on the East and West Coasts, **Robert L. Tiemann** has lived in St. Louis for the past thirty years and has written and edited numerous articles and journals for the Society for American Baseball Research (SABR).